# Beyond
# the Pattern

from *Threads*

# Beyond the Pattern

## Great Sewing Techniques for Clothing

from *Threads*

The Taunton Press

Cover photo: Amy Yanagi

Taunton
BOOKS & VIDEOS
*for fellow enthusiasts*

First printing: January 1995
Second printing: December 1995
Printed in the United States of America

A THREADS Book

THREADS® is a trademark of The Taunton Press, Inc.,
registered in the U.S. Patent and Trademark Office.

The Taunton Press
63 South Main Street
Box 5506
Newtown, CT 06470-5506

Library of Congress Cataloging-in-Publication Data

Beyond the pattern : great sewing techniques for clothing / from
    Threads.
        p.   cm.
    "A Threads book" — T.p. verso.
    Includes index.
    ISBN 1-56158-094-5
    1. Machine sewing.  2. Tailoring.  3. Tailoring (Women's).
4. Clothing and dress.  I. Threads magazine.
TT713.B45   1995                              94-37378
646.4 — dc20                                  CIP

# Contents

# Introduction

*t*he hallmark of a well-made garment is construction that is inconspicuous: seams don't ripple, hems are invisible, zippers don't gap, and facings don't show. The fabric, interfacing, and thread all work together to create a satisfying garment — one you can be proud of.

And, yes, *you* can pull all this together. Here, from the pages of *Threads* magazine, is advice from experts detailed with step-by-step instructions. You'll find the fundamental information you need on ease, bias, turn of the cloth, seam allowances, fabric preparation, and thread and interfacing selection. And you'll discover detailed instructions for all the essential applications — zippers, buttonholes, linings, pockets, collars, sleeves, and hems.

Whether you're just starting out or have sewn for years, you'll find techniques you can use again and again. And even more, as readers of *Threads* have come to expect, you'll be building a foundation that will benefit every future sewing project.

*Suzanne LaRosa, publisher*

# Mechanical, Electronic, or Computerized?

## Here's what each type of modern sewing machine can do for you

*by Karen Morris*

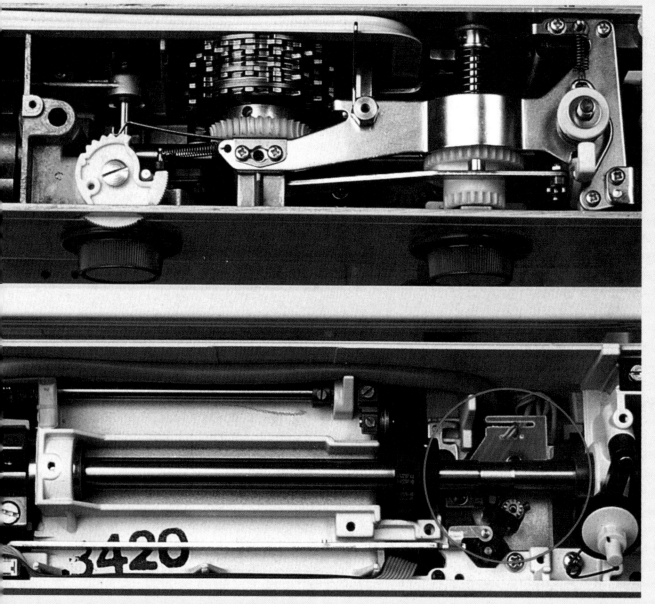

Linkages fill the head of a **mechanical sewing machine** (top left), connecting all movement to one motor. Eleven metal cams, one for each stitch pattern, are mounted side by side (center of machine).

**Computerization and multiple motors** eliminate many moving parts (bottom). The large center shaft controls the needle up/down movement. The flat shaft at the bottom connects a small stepping motor to the needle for side-to-side movement. The stepping motor is mounted underneath the small white gear and gold plate in the circled area. The green area is a small circuit board that controls the step motor.

*U*ntil recently, I was content with my reliable 1968 all-mechanical zig-zag-model sewing machine for sewing an occasional comforter cover or to make a few shoulder pads. Then I got the itch to buy a new machine.

I thought that what I needed was a top-of-the-line mechanical machine. The idea of computer circuitry replacing most of the gears and mechanical parts wasn't appealing. And what about all that plastic that manufacturers are using instead of metal? But still, I decided I ought to learn what electronics and computerization are all about. Over the next several months I spoke with repair people and technicians who are knowledgeable about the three kinds of machines available to home sewers today: mechanical, electronic, and computerized. I asked about the features the machines offer and their reliability. I also spoke to people who sewed on electronic and computerized machines.

Well, I eventually bought a computerized sewing machine, which is so user friendly that I'd feel comfortable letting my six-year-old learn to sew on it. I have come to realize that computerized and electronic machines have some wonderful features. They can actually save you time, be a lot of fun to run, and make it easier to sew details, such as buttonholes, accurately. Computerized machines, however, aren't necessarily for everyone. You may not need the features they offer, and they're more expensive than mechanical or electronic machines (you're paying for a lot of development and programming). To help you in your own search, here are the basics I learned about how each type of machine works.

### Starting with mechanical

Mechanical, electronic, and computerized machines all form the basic stitch in the same way: A needle carries thread down through the fabric, where the thread is caught and looped around the bobbin mechanism, then pulled back up by a take-up lever, while the feed dog moves the fabric into position for the next stitch. (For more on how a stitch is formed, see the article on pp. 16-18.) This is where the similarity ends because what moves the needle, bobbin, take-up lever and feed dog varies greatly.

In mechanical machines, all movement is initiated by a single motor connected to the needle and feed dog by cams and levers. A cam is a flat wheel with a ridged edge, as you can see in the upper part of the photo on the facing page. Every stitch pattern—straight, zig-zag, blind hem, overlock, scallop—has its own cam. As a cam turns (actually, all the cams turn together on a shaft), its uneven surface pushes nearby levers into position, which eventually causes the needle to move in the pattern of a particular stitch.

Functions such as tension, stitch length, and stitch width are manually selected by turning a dial. Once you set the stitch width and length, that's what you get for the stitch pattern, even for a decorative stitch like a scallop, as shown in the photo below. However, because you make width and length adjustments by turning a dial, you can usually make infinitely fine adjustments.

All-mechanical sewing machines are operated by a foot pedal/motor combination that produces power in proportion to how far down you press the foot pedal. The farther down you press, the more electricity the motor gets, so the more power it produces. When you sew slowly, the motor receives less electricity and has less power, which makes sewing slowly on heavy fabric like denim more difficult; just when you need more power, you have less.

The skill of the machine operator determines the degree of sewing precision and control. Let's say I'm topstitching the point of a collar and I want to pivot at the point, which means I have to stop exactly at the point with the needle down. I might sew fairly fast up to within two or three stitches of the collar point, then sew slowly or even turn the hand wheel by hand so I stop with the needle down precisely where I want it.

Another example of how the sewer's skill affects the quality of sewing is making a buttonhole. Many mechanical machines offer a sequence on the stitch selector dial for making a buttonhole, but the sewer must mark the ends of each buttonhole and turn the dial to control the stitching sequence so the buttonholes end up the same size.

### Electronics adds control

The lines between machine types start blurring when we get to electronic features and computerization because they often go hand in hand. I define an electronic machine in this article as one that still has one motor, and cams and linkages, but is enhanced by electronic control. Electronics means that some of the mechanical features, like the position of the needle (up or down), are measured by an electrified sensor—an electronic eye, perhaps a switch. The sensor feeds back information to you (turning on a warning light, for example) or to the motor.

Electronics adds precision and control that would require a lot more parts or be impossible to do mechanically. The sensors and control relieves the sewer of having to manually control different functions, and thus the machine requires somewhat less skill to operate.

Electronic machines generally have some or all of the following features:
• Automatic needle stop in the up or down position
• Even power at all speeds
• Slow or fast sewing speed option
• Low bobbin warning

Although all the major functions of an electronic machine are mechanical, a circuit board (a computer part containing pathways for electrical impulses) controls the special electronic features. The low bobbin thread warning signal operates, for example, with a beam of infrared or natural white light projected onto a clear plastic bobbin (photo on p. 11). When the bobbin is full, the thread interrupts the beam of light; as the bobbin empties, the light beam passes through the bobbin and activates a light receiver on the other side, which gives a signal to the computer to turn on the low bobbin warning signal.

### Computerization offers programming

As the sewing machine companies added more and more innovations and stitch patterns to mechanical and electronically enhanced mechanical machines, the advanced models became complicated, intricate, and packed with moving parts. According to one of the repair people I spoke with, some of the most complex machines were overly sensitive to being

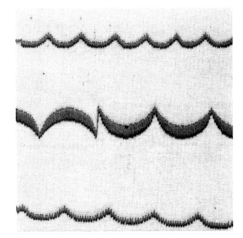

*The scallop stitching of a mechanical machine (top and bottom rows) has a constant width and length, once set. In contrast, the stitch width of the computerized version varies from short to long (center), and the push of a button flips the pattern.*

even slightly out of adjustment. Some of the internal settings were so exacting that they had to be adjusted by an expert with special equipment. To simplify the mechanics, manufacturers have been adding motors for different directions of needle and feed dog movement—needle up/down and side to side, and feed dog forward and backward and side to side. This has eliminated many of the complex linkages (lower machine, photo on p. 8) needed to operate a machine from one motor. And to coordinate the movement and synchronization of all the motors, they added a computer.

The advantage of computerization is that a sequence of steps, as simple as those for making a buttonhole, can be programmed and saved in the computer's memory. Instead of requiring a complex cam, every type of stitch pattern is analyzed and broken down into a programmable series of distinct movements.

A computerized machine uses special electronic motors, called stepping motors. A stepping motor can rotate both clockwise and counterclockwise, unlike the motors in mechanical machines, which are generally meant to turn in only one direction. Stepping motors can turn in precise, discrete steps, or partial rotations; in fact, if you turn the gear of a stepping motor gently with your fingers, you can feel a series of distinct clicks. The amount of motor movement is proportional to the amount of stitch width and length: The width of a zigzag stitch can be as narrow as the motor step is small, for example. Wider zigzags are the result of wide motor swings.

Unlike the infinitely fine adjustments that you can make by turning the dial of a mechanical machine, the movements created by a step motor must be adjusted in increments. This is not really a disadvantage, because the increments can be quite small—.1mm for stitch width and .05mm for length, for example. The size of incre-

ments is certainly a detail of a computerized machine that you'll want to check, because they vary widely between models.

The stepping motor takes its orders from electrical signals coming from a main circuit board, which contains the stitch programs, electronic functions, and the memory that stores all the programs. Most computerized machines have buttons, rather than dials. When you press a button to select a stitch on the control panel of a computer machine, you are selecting a program and sending a signal to the circuit board. Some computerized machines can store programs for hundreds of stitch patterns, including stitches you create yourself.

Computerized machines offer the features of the electronic ones and other features available only because of the step motors and programming:
- Ability to flip patterns to create mirror images of stitch patterns.
- Ability to store the dimensions of but-

# How to test a sewing machine

### by Gale Grigg Hazen

To many people, testing a machine can appear to be an intimidating experience. Here's a way to test a machine and find a good dealer at the same time. I'd recommend trying several brands (not just different models of the same brand) just for the sake of comparison. Each machine has its own feel and touch, and personal preference will have a lot to do with how much you'll enjoy working on the machine you finally buy.

New machines have so many stitches that you'll probably only be able to test a few. Be sure to test the basic stitches you'll need for a garment, such as a straight stitch, zigzag, buttonholes, and overlock. (To make sure you check the machine's basic equipment, I recommend taking along the checklist from *Threads* No. 35, p. 56.)

**Fabric samples**—You'll need pairs of 18- by 3-in. fabric samples of different weights and fibers; you usually sew two layers together, so test with two layers. This length will allow you to adjust the stitch width, length, and tension, and the width allows you to do several stitch runs spaced so a previous line of stitching won't affect the stitch quality of the run you're on.

Include the following fabrics: knit (any fiber type), silky lightweight polyester, silk charmeuse, heavy fabric with a coating—like a rubber-backed upholstery fabric or nylon of backpack weight—and plain 100 percent cotton like muslin. A ¼ yd. of each fabric will be enough to test several machine brands.

The knit will tell you how well a machine performs on stretchy fabrics. The results on the polyester will tell you how well the top and bobbin threads interlock, while the slippery silk tells you how well the feed dog and foot hold and move the fabric. Heavy, coated fabric tests how strong the top tension is and whether the machine can pull the thread so it doesn't get stuck in loops on the underside of the fabric.

I would also take along the legs from a pair of old jeans to test the machine's ability to penetrate thick, densely woven fabric, particularly across the welt seam of the outer or inner leg at the hem.

**Thread and needles**—A knowledgeable dealer and dedicated sewer realizes that making perfect stitches takes a balance of thread, needle, fabric, and tension. Such a dealer stocks a good selection of quality thread and needles available for sale and testing.

However, if you'd like to be prepared, bring a selection of fine to heavy needles, and the following threads: a midweight polyester (Mettler's 100 or Gutterman's All Purpose are good); size 50/3 100 percent mercerized cotton, like Mettler; 60/2 100 percent cotton (this may be labeled as embroidery thread); and a heavy-duty poly or cotton. I'd use the midweight poly on the knit for stretch, fine cotton for the silk and polyester silky, regular cotton for the muslin, and heavy duty for the upholstery fabric.

**The test**—Start by asking the dealer to demonstrate the machine. Tell the dealer your budget up front; I'd beware if the dealer insists on demonstrating on a much higher priced model after you've indicated your price range. (If the dealer just wants to show you a video, that's probably not a dealer you're going to get great service from.) The dealer may go through the basics using a loosely woven, starched white fabric called demo cloth. The loose weave makes it easy for the needle to penetrate and the stiffness prevents the fabric from being pulled downward and upward by the needle, so the stitching never puckers.

Then pull out your samples and ask the dealer to run through several stitches on each one. Even if a machine is advertised as having a self-adjusting tension, the reality is that you may have to adjust the tension for fabrics outside of the norm—fine fabrics like batiste or thick fabrics like batted quilting, for example. Hopefully you'll find the dealer willing and eager to change needles and thread to match your samples.

Now it's time for you to accustom yourself to the machine. If you can't make acceptable stitches, don't be shy about asking the dealer to show you how.

Hang on to your samples and label them. After you've tested several brands, take a look at all the samples, compare them, then make your decision.

---

*Gale Grigg Hazen, the author of* Owner's Guide to Sewing Machines, Sergers, and Knitting Machines *(Chilton, 1989), runs a sewing school in Saratoga, CA.*

tonholes, so that once you've made one buttonhole, the rest will be identical (no marking and careful control needed.)
• Lots of buttonholes (keyhole, stretch, straight).
• Stitch patterns with varying width and length in the pattern (photo on p. 9).
• Wider stitch patterns (often the result of a step motor that moves the feed dog from side to side).
• Multicolor stitches.

I would like to add a caution at this point about embroidery. Even a computerized machine is a sewing machine, not an industrial embroidery machine. Up to as many as ten industrial embroidery machines, each dedicated to a special stitch, may have been used to produce a design that you see on a ready-to-wear blouse that may not be reproducible at home. If you plan to do a lot of machine embroidery, examine each machine not just for number and combinations of stitches, but for quality of stitches and multicolor capability as well.

If you go shopping for a computerized machine, also keep in mind that all computer machines are not created equal. Some are much more user friendly than others and the only way you can see which one you like is to try them out.

## Concerning plastic

Plastic parts are used in nearly all machines these days. Before you become alarmed, here's a bit of background information that calmed me. To avoid frequent oiling and maintenance in home sewing machines, moving parts made of steel were often paired with adjacent parts of a softer metal such as bronze. Today the bronze has been replaced in many machines by Lexan, a tough, durable nylon also used to make nose cones for the space shuttle. If you're worried that the machine you want contains cheap and nondurable plastic, ask the dealer to explain what type of plastic is in the machine.

## Repairs and warranties

You might still be wondering, as I was, whether you can trust the reliability of an electronic or computerized machine. Repair people admit that earlier computerization had its problems. Now that computerized machines have been around for a while, and redesigned and improved many times, the early problems have been solved. Computer machines today have about the same rate of repair as mechanical machines. In fact, many of the new machines are modularly built, and snap apart for easier, faster repairs. Some repairs take one-fourth the time of the same repair on a mechanical ma-

chine, which represents a significant savings in labor costs. Warranties for parts and labor vary widely among companies though, so it makes sense to buy as long a warranty as you can for both.

Many people mistakenly believe that their mechanical sewing machine's 20- or 25-year warranty covers the entire machine for 20 to 25 years. Actually this kind of warranty is usually limited and ensures only that the machine will be free from defects in materials and workmanship. A typical 20-year warranty covers replacement of the body of the machine if it cracks, but does not cover any problems due to ordinary wear and tear.

Manufacturers' warranties on parts in all types of inexpensive machines, including the circuit board, are often for only 90 days; more commonly they range from two to five years for more expensive machines. Manufacturers' warranties on labor, which cover the work needed for a repair, vary between zero and two years. Many dealers will extend these warranties on models that they find to be relatively trouble-free.

The price of circuit boards and other computer parts have fallen significantly

---

*. . . all computer machines are not created equal. Some are much more user friendly than others.*

---

in the past few years and will continue to decrease as production techniques improve, just as they have in the home computer market. For now, though, replacing a step motor or circuit board represents a major expense, and no one quite knows how long a circuit board can last. Dealers say if you have a good board, it should last for many years. It is possible to get a bad board—a circuit board which has a short life. Sometimes a problem will develop soon after you begin to sew, but it may not become apparent until the machine has been used for a thousand hours. A circuit board can cost as much as $125 and take from ten minutes to more than an hour to replace; if the parts and labor aren't covered by a warranty, this repair could cost you $200. Thus, it makes sense to buy a computerized machine with as long a warranty on parts and labor as possible.

**Electronic bobbin fullness indicator:** *Light from a bulb (at scissors' point) projects on the side of a clear bobbin. When the bobbin runs low, the light goes to the back of the bobbin case, where it hits a sensor. The sensor triggers a warning light, a beep, or a visual message.*

The longevity of computerized machines is not yet known, because the machines are relatively new, but the manufacturers believe they will last longer than mechanical machines; they have fewer moving parts with less to go wrong. Computer machines do not require oiling except in the bobbin area, although neither do many current mechanical machines, which are now self-lubricating.

## Deciding what you need

Before you buy, examine how and when you will use the machine, and for what tasks. (For some tips about testing a machine, see "How to test a sewing machine" on the facing page.)

I decided to buy a two-year-old computerized machine with a price tag I could afford. The friendliness and ease of use made me feel at home with my machine after only a few hours of sewing.

Many sewers say they don't use their machine's embroidery stitches much after the initial novelty wears off. That may happen to me after I've had my machine for a while. But for now, I've been embroidering my daughter's name on her cloth napkin for school, and stitching dinosaurs on the new knee patch for my son's jeans. When I press my machine's foot pedal to the floor, the machine sews like lightning and it's very quiet; it sounds as if it's whispering.

Do we want computer machines? The answer is different for each of us, because our needs are different. But personally, I find the technology irresistible. □

---

*Karen Morris repaired clocks, taught mathematics, and designed knits prior to joining* Threads *as an assistant editor.*

# Perfecting the Straight Stitch

## When you use a stitch as often as you do this one, why not do it right?

*by Gale Grigg Hazen*

Chances are, if you're working on a machine-sewing project, you're going to use a straight stitch—and you want the stitch to look good. An ideal straight stitch lies flat, holds firm, and does not pucker the fabric. These qualities don't sound like a lot to ask for but sometimes seem impossible to obtain.

The first step towards mastering the art of the straight stitch is understanding how the stitch is made (see the drawing on the facing page). It's also important to be aware of the variables that can affect stitch quality, such as the choice of throat plate and foot, stitch length, upper and bobbin thread tension, and even the thickness of the fabric. And finally, you've got to match your straight stitch settings to the task at hand, whether basting, easing, or topstitching. Let's cover the critical points of information you need, one by one.

### What is a stitch?

When a sewing machine makes a stitch, the upper and lower threads twist around each other in a knot and hold the fabric layers together, ideally with the knot centered between the layers (see the drawing on the facing page). The thread that shows on the surface should lie flat without wavering.

You should note that there's a difference between wavering and the slight natural curve of the thread between each stitch. A waver is irregular and does not always curve in the same direction. The natural curve in a straight stitch, caused by the upper thread emerging from one side of a knot and entering the next knot on the other side, always slants in the same direction, as shown in the photo on the facing page. This curve will be less noticeable when you sew with a straight-stitch foot and throat plate, because the narrow

holes in the foot and plate support the fabric all around the area where the needle enters the fabric, reducing any unwanted fabric movement.

A sewing machine that does straight stitching only, with a side-loading bobbin and a needle that threads from the side (such as the Singer Featherweight and most simple treadle machines), makes straight stitches with less built-in curve than a zigzag machine. Since the eye of the needle in a straight-stitch-only machine faces to the side, the upper thread doesn't twist as much to pass around the bobbin thread, which results in a straighter stitch.

Regardless of whether you have a straight-stitch-only or a fancy 200-stitch electronic machine, there are a few minor adjustments you can make that will improve your stitch quality, including altering the straight-stitch length and settings to better perform specific tasks.

### Analyzing stitch problems

There are many variables working together to create a machine stitch, so the cause of a poor-quality stitch can be difficult to pinpoint. If you're not satisfied with your stitch quality, first look at where the knots lie in relation to the fabric surface, then check the thread quality, feed dog, and choice of presser foot.

**Location of knots—***If the knots show above the fabric surface and the fabric doesn't pucker,* the lower tension could be too loose. Loose lower tension is usually caused by an incorrect bobbin tension setting, which can be corrected by adjusting the screw on the bobbin case (see *Threads* No. 53, p. 20). Loose lower tension can also be the result of the thread feeding through the bobbin tension mechanism incorrectly.

*If the knots show above the fabric surface and the fabric*

From *Threads* magazine (August 1994) 54:38-41

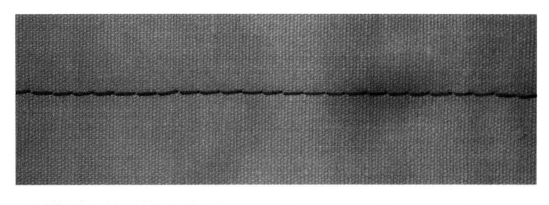

### Natural curve of a straight stitch

*All straight stitching starts slightly due to the way it's made.*

Top thread emerges from one side of knot . . .

. . . and enters the other side of the next knot

. . . causing a slight curve.

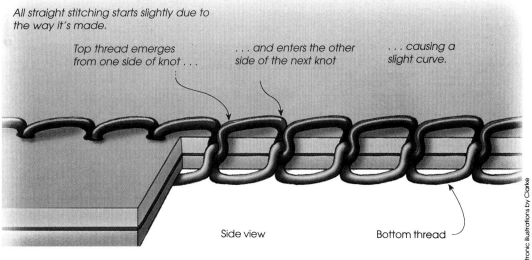

Side view

Bottom thread

Electronic illustrations by Clarke

*puckers*, the upper tension could be too tight. Too-tight upper tension can be caused by an incorrect tension setting, which can be corrected simply by adjusting the tension dial. Too-tight upper tension can also be caused by a snag somewhere in the thread path between spool and needle, or can occur if you use thread that's too thick for the eye of the needle.

*If the knots lie on the underside of the fabric and the fabric doesn't pucker,* the upper tension could be too loose. This can be caused either by an incorrect tension setting (check the dial) or by the thread feeding through the upper tension mechanism incorrectly.

*If the knots lie below the fabric and the fabric puckers,* the lower tension could be too tight. To fix this, adjust the screw on the bobbin case.

If these adjustments fail to correct a tension problem, the machine may need professional repair.

**Choice of thread**—The type of thread you choose also affects the quality of your stitches. My rule is to avoid threads that stretch, especially when you're sewing on lightweight fabrics. Poor-quality polyester or cotton-wrapped polyester thread can lengthen during sewing and then contract in the seam, causing puckers. To test the thread, stretch a 12-in.-long piece; a high-quality thread has very little stretch. Spun polyesters, made from short fibers, often stretch quite a bit, while the more expensive extruded polyesters, made from a single filament of polyester, do not.

Poor-quality thread can also cause irregular stitches. If the thread has lumps, bumps, and skinny spots, it cannot travel through the tension mechanism smoothly and will not produce a good stitch.

When you sew thin cotton or silky fabrics, your choice of thread size becomes an im-

portant factor in stitch quality. Since the stitching looks best when the knot is buried inside the fabric layers, the knot needs to be smaller than the thickness of the fabric. For a good seam in a thin fabric, you'll need to use a fine thread, such as size 60/2.

Quilting has its own special thread needs. Because quilting requires many short seams, quilters pack thousands of stitches into a small area. For smooth results, quilters need to use a flexible thread. Many quilters insist on sewing with cotton fabrics because cotton presses well and is pliable; for the same reason, they should sew with cotton thread. Seams sewn with cotton are smooth and flat.

**Feed dog problems**—A poorly constructed or misaligned feed dog can cause uneven stitches. Many machines made during the 1960s have rubber feed dogs that are now drying out and wearing un-

evenly. If the teeth on the feed dog are irregular or rough, they do not grip the fabric firmly or feed evenly. And if the two sides of the feed dog do not move smoothly and straight, the fabric will fight the feed dog, causing a wavy line of stitching. If you have to fight with the fabric to get a straight line of stitching, your feed dog probably needs repair or replacement.

**Selecting a presser foot**—The shape of the bottom of the foot, which presses the fabric against the feed dog, helps the machine make good stitches. Sewing with the wrong foot for your fabric can result in irregular stitches and a wavy seamline. Some feet, for example, have a groove on the bottom to allow them to ride smoothly over thread build-up, as in satin stitching, or to permit a thick fabric to move under the foot easily. If a foot with this groove is used for straight stitching on a smooth

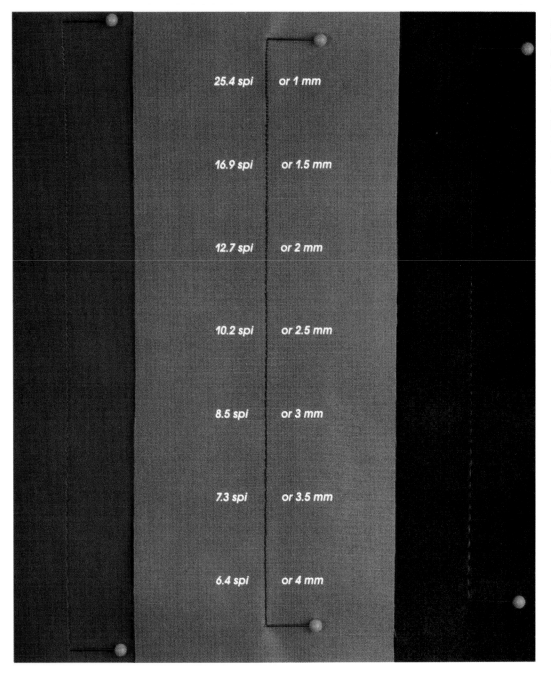

| 25.4 spi | or 1 mm |
| 16.9 spi | or 1.5 mm |
| 12.7 spi | or 2 mm |
| 10.2 spi | or 2.5 mm |
| 8.5 spi | or 3 mm |
| 7.3 spi | or 3.5 mm |
| 6.4 spi | or 4 mm |

**Stitch length changes with fabric:** *The length of straight stitches on medium-weight cotton fabric (center) can be your standard for comparison. The same stitch-length setting creates shorter stitches in thick or nubby fabrics such as the velvet on the right and longer stitches in thin or slippery fabrics such as the chiffon at left.*

or thin fabric, the foot will not make firm contact with the fabric, so the fabric may jerk and feed unevenly.

For precise stitching, especially on fine, thin fabrics like the fine cottons used in heirloom sewing, you need even and precise feeding. A special fine-fabric foot, which has a wide, flat bottom, improves the stitch quality by making firm contact with the feed dog for even feeding and decreased fabric flutter. Fine fabrics also require looser upper and lower tension to help prevent puckering.

For any type of sewing, make sure the foot is wide enough to cover the feed dog, preferably on both sides. A wide feed dog may not contact some feet adequately to hold the fabric firmly and feed evenly.

A rough spot on the bottom of the foot or on the throat plate can cause uneven feeding. Even the tiniest burr can catch on the fabric. Every time the fabric catches, it jerks, causing uneven stitches.

## Understanding stitch length

Another factor that affects the appearance and performance of straight stitches is

their length. On sewing machines, stitch length is usually expressed in one of two ways: either as stitches per inch (spi); or as millimeters between stitches or knots, usually 0 to 4 (or even longer on newer machines), with the standard at 2.5 mm. But getting the stitch length you want is not just a matter of setting a knob or a number. You need to understand the relationship between the feed dog and the fabric.

When the sewing machine makes a stitch, the feed dog rises and moves a distance determined by the stitch length

setting. The stitch length mechanism is designed to give the prescribed length stitch on a medium-weight, firm fabric. However, this same motion of the feed dog will give different stitch lengths on other fabrics. The amount of resistance of the fabric (in the form of thickness, nap, or slipperiness) affects the distance the feed dog movement pushes the fabric.

A thick, rough fabric, for example, is hard to move, so the distance covered at a given stitch-length setting is less, and the stitches are short (see the photo above). A thin or slippery fabric moves farther with the same amount of feed dog movement, which results in longer stitches. If the stitches appear too short or too long at a chosen setting, adjust the setting to give the desired stitch length for the fabric you're using.

The fact that a fine, thin fabric moves farther at a given stitch length setting contributes to puckering. When the distance that the fabric moves is greater than the length of thread the machine feeds out for each stitch, the short thread will pull up the fabric and cause puckering. Shortening the stitch length will enable you to produce smoother seams.

If your sewing machine stitch-length knob is poorly marked, you can sew a test swatch of straight stitches on a piece of medium-weight cotton, such as the one shown at center in the photo on the facing page. Measure each different stitch length on the swatch, and use a fine-point permanent marker to record the lengths directly on the stitch-length knob.

A smooth start-up and consistent sewing speed also help the feed dog maintain an even stitch length. Rapid, uneven starts and stops don't allow the feed dog to grasp the fabric firmly. Instead, the teeth slide over the fabric, resulting in shorter-than-normal stitches at the beginning and end of a seam.

## Special uses for straight stitching

Pattern instructions often call for special straight stitches. Following are tips that will give you better results with some specific stitches.

**Staystitching**—Often recommended in pattern instructions on one layer of fabric along necklines and sleeve openings, staystitching helps to prevent stretching and distortion of bias areas. Because it is sewn on a single layer, staystitching often puckers the fabric. Using a shorter-

than-normal stitch length will improve stitch quality and reduce puckering.

**Reinforcing**—A line of reinforcing stitches is often recommended on single and double layers to strengthen the seamline. On a single layer, the reinforcement stitching helps to prevent raveling or tearing when a clip ends on the seamline. On a double layer, reinforcement stitching next to the seamline can prevent tearing at a stress point, such as on an armhole or crotch seam. Always use a short stitch length (such as 1.5 to 2 mm) to achieve maximum strength.

**Basting**—Basting must hold layers of fabric together temporarily and be easy to rip out. A long stitch length creates the fewest knots to rip but often causes the fabric to pucker. The solution is to decrease the upper tension, which reduces puckering and causes the knots to fall to the bottom, making stitches easy to remove—just pull the bobbin thread.

**Gathering**—Gathering stitches are also sewn on the longest setting. For stitching that's easy to gather, increase the upper tension. This causes the tension mechanism to hold firmly onto the thread, reducing the amount of thread that enters the stitch, while the feed dog pulls through the maximum amount of fabric. The fabric gathers and the knots pull to the top, allowing the fullness to be adjusted easily by pulling the top thread.

**Easing**—To sew shape into a garment, it is often necessary to stitch two layers of different lengths together, such as an armscye to a sleeve cap, without puckers. This is called *easing*. To coax the longer layer to the length of the shorter layer, you need to compress the longer layer slightly at the seamline before stitching the two layers

**Unbalanced stitching has its uses**
*You can intentionally unbalance the tension to give ideal results for special types of straight stitching.*

**Basting**
*Using a long stitch, decrease upper tension to reduce puckering and bring knots to bottom for easy stitch removal.*

**Gathering**
*Using a long stitch, increase upper tension so fabric starts to gather and knots pull to top for easy adjusting of fullness.*

**Easing**
*First ease one layer, using a medium-length stitch and increasing upper tension slightly. Then assemble two layers with longer side down.*

together. If you sew gathering stitches on the longer layer, the finished seam will often have tiny pleats or gathers instead of appearing smooth. Rather than gathering, ease smoothly by using a medium stitch length with the upper thread tension slightly increased. The seam will shorten slightly without pleating. Then when you're ready to stitch the two layers together, sew the seam with the longer layer against the feed dog. This allows the machine's tendency to pull the bottom layer through faster than the top to work to your advantage.

## Don't forget to test

Before sewing, you probably test interfacing on your fabric, but you may not think to test your stitching. Always test stitch quality by sewing a sample with the needle, thread, foot, stitch length, and thread tension you plan to use. Only then can you confidently begin each project knowing that your sewing will be successful. □

*Gale Grigg Hazen teaches sewing workshops throughout the country. Her article on ease appears on pp. 46-49.*

# Why Stitches Skip and Fabric Puckers

## How to improve stitch quality and start loving your sewing machine

*by Gale Grigg Hazen*

**m**ost sewers, even very accomplished ones, don't really understand how sewing machines work, and it's not because our machines have become so elaborate. I'm talking about how a stitch is formed; what happens when the needle goes up and down and the feed dogs move? In fact what happens is the same on every sort of machine, from treadles to the computer-controlled wonders. Once you have a clear idea of what's going on, I think you'll find that you can make better use of your machine, keeping ordinary tasks trouble-free and unmysterious, and even letting the machine handle much of your easing, gathering, and basting.

### Making thread loops

Although machine stitches attempt to duplicate hand stitches, there's no comparison between your handmade single-thread stitch and a machine-made two-thread stitch. The drawings below trace the machine process.

**Thread movement**–The first thing to realize about a machine-made stitch is how much thread movement is involved. If you follow the path of the little blue dot on the thread in the drawings just mentioned, you'll notice how it moves from one side of the needle hole to the other and back with every stitch. In fact, depending on the length of your stitch, that marked section of thread will slide back and forth through the needle and the fabric as often as 60 times before coming to rest in a stitch.

Before we examine why, I think you can see right away why you should choose your thread for smoothness and strength, and carefully match it to the size of your needle. I never skimp on quality thread; I choose all-cotton when I want my seams to look great, or long-staple polyester when the strength of the seam is more important than its looks. Unless you're into decorative stitchery, I suggest you settle on a few brands of thread that work for you and are easy to get, and stick to them. There's much more to say about thread, and I plan to devote an entire article to it in an upcoming issue.

**Clearing the bobbin**–The reason the thread moves so much is that the top

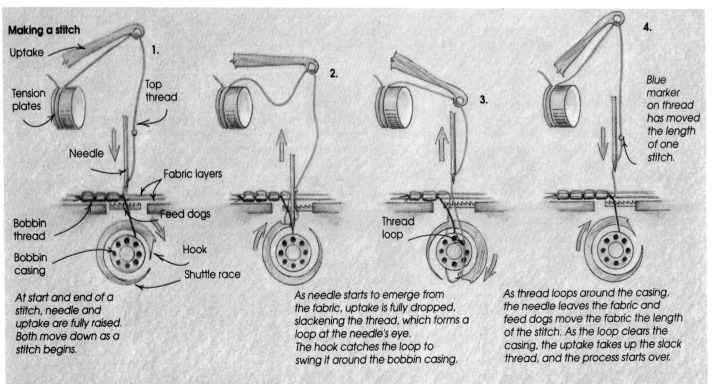

**Making a stitch**

Uptake

Tension plates

Top thread

Needle

Fabric layers

Feed dogs

Bobbin thread

Bobbin casing

Hook

Shuttle race

1.

At start and end of a stitch, needle and uptake are fully raised. Both move down as a stitch begins.

2.

As needle starts to emerge from the fabric, uptake is fully dropped, slackening the thread, which forms a loop at the needle's eye.
The hook catches the loop to swing it around the bobbin casing.

3.

Thread loop

As thread loops around the casing, the needle leaves the fabric and feed dogs move the fabric the length of the stitch. As the loop clears the casing, the uptake takes up the slack thread, and the process starts over.

4.

Blue marker on thread has moved the length of one stitch.

Illustrations by Christopher Clapp

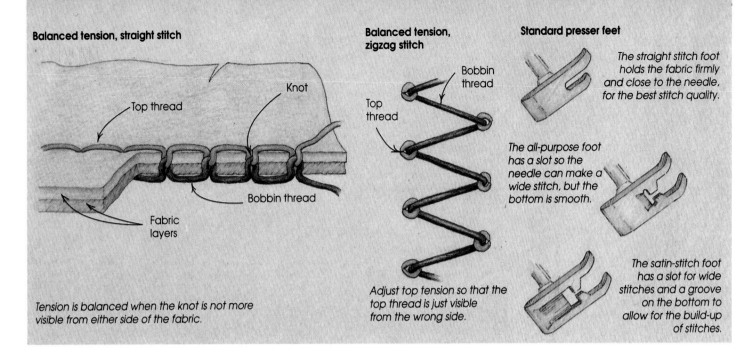

**Balanced tension, straight stitch**

Top thread

Knot

Bobbin thread

Fabric layers

Tension is balanced when the knot is not more visible from either side of the fabric.

**Balanced tension, zigzag stitch**

Bobbin thread

Top thread

Adjust top tension so that the top thread is just visible from the wrong side.

**Standard presser feet**

The straight stitch foot holds the fabric firmly and close to the needle, for the best stitch quality.

The all-purpose foot has a slot so the needle can make a wide stitch, but the bottom is smooth.

The satin-stitch foot has a slot for wide stitches and a groove on the bottom to allow for the build-up of stitches.

thread must loop completely around the bobbin each time a stitch is formed, which requires about 2 in. to 4 in. of loose thread. Where does the loop come from? Let's return to the drawings on p. 16 and look more closely.

Notice how the movements of the *needle*, the *uptake* (the moving arm you thread through at the top of every machine), and the *shuttle race* (the mechanism surrounding the bobbin and holding it in place) are carefully synchronized to create a thread loop and move it around the bobbin. If for any reason the little thread loop (see drawing 2) fails to form, or the hook on the shuttle race fails to catch it, you get a skipped stitch. Drawing 3 should explain why trying to remove the fabric before the uptake is completely raised won't work, even if the needle is all the way up: The loop is still wrapped around the bobbin casing.

### Setting tensions

Setting and adjusting top and bottom tensions isn't hard, and when you've got the confidence to do it, you'll get much better results from your machine. Machines with "Universal" or "Automatic" tensions have superb tension mechanisms that permit a wide range of variables without adjustment, but their settings can be, and sometimes need to be, overridden. Sewers who want to be in control should feel confident to do so.

**Bobbin tension**—The bobbin thread merely has to stay put while the top thread goes around it, so its tension mechanism is simple: a screw holding a spring-steel tension plate against the thread is all it takes. It's usually better to set this for your most usual combination of thread and fabric and

forget it, except as described below, because you can weaken the spring with too much adjusting. If you use lots of different or heavy threads in the bobbin, get another case and mark it as the looser one.

When you do want or need to adjust bobbin tension, start with cautious turns of the set screw, making tiny shifts to the right to tighten, or to the left to loosen; a quarter turn is a major change, so restrain yourself. Test the results, and fine-tune with the top tension setting.

**Top tension**—The top thread traces an elaborate path from spool to needle; it's important to realize that each step along the way contributes to the top tension, not just the setting on the tension dial. Tension is the total resistance against the thread as it travels through the machine from spool to needle. The dial merely fine-tunes the resistance in order to control the top thread's longer movement, so if your tension's way off, check the whole path.

Inside the tension mechanism are separating plates between which the thread passes. Newer machines have three plates, so there's a separate space for each of two threads. Lowering the presser foot engages the top tension mechanism by pressing the plates together; the tension dial controls the amount of pressure that gets applied. The proper tension is whatever setting balances the bobbin tension so that the knots that hold top and bottom threads together in a stitch are equally spaced between the top and bottom of the fabric layers, as shown in the familiar drawing above left, *and* so that there's no seam puckering. For most situations, dial up a zigzag stitch and adjust it to look like the one in the drawing above center; this is the easiest way to see

the balance between the threads.

The fabric you're stitching is a major contributor to this happy balance. As you sew, the top thread is attached to the tension path at one end, and to the just-made stitch on the other. To make the next stitch, the machine will pull the thread it needs from whichever end offers the least resistance.

If the fabric is soft, pulling thread from the last stitch could be easier, resulting in puckers. You can shorten the stitch length, so that there's less fabric to give between each stitch, and you can loosen top and bottom tensions equally so the resistance from the spool end is less. If you loosen just the top tension, the knots will fall to the bobbin side of the stitch, which looks better than puckering, but weakens the stitch. Sewing on thin, soft fabrics like charmeuse, chiffon, crepe de chine, Swiss batiste, and voile is about the only situation for which I'd recommend that you adjust your bobbin tensions away from your preferred "normal."

**Tension settings for specialized stitches**—The tension dial can also be used to make some sewing activities easier. When you need to *gather*, but the exact amount of gathering isn't critical, try increasing the top tension and setting the stitch length to maximum. The machine will hold back the thread, so that the feed dogs pull the single layer of fabric farther than the amount of thread the machine has allowed. What's the result? Deep, regularly spaced puckers, or gathers. Experiment with different settings; you won't hurt the machine. I prefer this to using a gathering foot, which can cause skipped stitches. To *baste* without puckers, reduce the tension to half the normal setting. In addition to no puckers, the knots will all fall to the back, and you'll be able to pull the bobbin thread out easily to remove the basting. When you're *satin stitching* to appliqué or to make buttonholes, reduce the thread tension slightly so the bobbin thread isn't seen, and to lessen the puckering.

## Presser foot basics

As needle and thread move up and down through the fabric, the fabric naturally tries to move with it, and if the presser foot doesn't hold the fabric securely, that's just what happens. If the fabric moves up with the needle, the little loop shown in drawing 2 (p. 16) doesn't form, the hook misses it, and the stitch gets skipped. This is why it's hard to stitch so close to a fabric edge that the presser foot can't grab both sides; the fabric flutters up and down with the needle. Whenever possible, sew at least ½ in. from the edge and then trim away. This is also why you need to hold fabric tightly in a hoop and press it down against the throat plate if you're sewing without a presser foot, for embroidery or darning.

Most people evaluate a presser foot by looking at the top of the foot, but the part of the foot that has the most contact with the fabric is the bottom. If you compare the most-used sewing feet, the straight-stitch/zigzag, or "all-purpose," foot and the satin-stitch foot, you'll see that a satin-stitch foot has a grooved bottom to allow the mound of thread created by the tight zigzag to move underneath without restriction, while the straight-stitch/zigzag foot is flat, in order to hold the material firmly and evenly across the whole width of the feed dogs. If you use the satin-stitch foot for normal sewing, you may get skipped stitches because the groove can allow fabric fluttering when there's no thread build-up.

There is one instance where the satin-stitch foot is appropriate for straight-stitch sewing. Soft, spongy fabrics like fleece get slightly spread out under the pressure of the foot, and this can cause stretched, wavy seams. If you switch to the satin-stitch foot, the groove will allow the fabric to keep its shape without stretching; the fabric is thick enough to prevent fluttering.

I recommend that you add a straight-stitch-only foot, like the one in the right-hand drawing on the previous page, to your collection. You'll get the best possible straight seams, because the fabric will be held as securely as possible around the needle. As long as you remember not to switch to zigzag without changing feet, you'll love it. If you can't find one, or you switch to zigzag often, try adjusting your needle position all the way to the right or left so that the zigzag slot will be providing support on three sides. Remember to change your seam-width markings to reflect the new needle position.

## Shifting fabric

While the needle and thread are swinging up and down, the feed dogs are waiting for just the right moment to make their move. They can't move at all while the needle's in the fabric because that would pull the needle off course. Once the fabric starts moving, however, a race begins between the layers of fabric; and the bottom layer always wins. The feed dogs have a better grasp on the bottom layer, so they push it a tiny bit farther than the top layer with each stitch. At the same time the presser foot pushes against the top layer and the cumulative effect is the bottom layer coming out shorter than the upper one.

This movement is called shift; it's increased by a number of factors. When more than two layers are being sewn, as in machine quilting, the upper and lower layers have less contact with each other and are more likely to move unequally. Any increase in drag on the top layer, such as letting your hands rest on the fabric, letting the fabric hang off the sewing surface, or sewing on extra-thick fabrics, will increase the shift. Soft, spongy, or stretchy fabrics, like sweater knits and hand-wovens, offer a lot of resistance against the foot. Very slick or slippery fabrics do not hold onto each other, so the bottom layer moves without taking the next layer with it.

To prevent or equalize the shift, try these techniques: Never sew more than two layers together at one time. If three or more layers are necessary, sew pairs first and then join the sets. With your fingers on both sides of the foot, stretch the fabric equally to either side and allow the fabric to feed steadily and evenly. Use a walking foot, available for most machines from local dealers; whether it's built-in or a separate attachment, this foot duplicates (over a smaller area) the motion of the feed dogs on the top layer. It's especially helpful on quilts. Every six inches, or more often as necessary, lift the foot and smooth back the fabric bubble that is created by the foot, shoving the top layer forward. This helps a great deal on knit fabrics. You can also hold just the bottom layer, letting the top rest free as you guide them both under the needle. The increased drag on the bottom will equalize the movement of the layers. Hand basting will eliminate shift completely, but pin basting will merely slow it down. If it's important to eliminate shift, take the time to baste.

You can also use this shift tendency to your advantage. Whenever one side of a seam must be eased in against the other, put the longer side against the feed dogs and allow the machine to do the easing.

## Fewer and fewer puckers

Of all sewing machine irritations, puckered seams are the most frequent and the most likely to be fixable by the knowledgeable home sewer. In addition to what's already been described, here are the most common reasons for puckers: The "knot" where the threads cross on a machine-sewn seam belongs within the fabric, but if the thread is thicker than the fabric, the knot is so bulky that it displaces the remaining fabric. The cumulative effect is a bumpy seam that appears puckered. Standard-weight cotton thread can cause puckers when it is initially sewn in, but the natural fiber will often press flat; a test will determine if this is the case. For very fine fabrics like crepe de chine or cotton batiste use extra-fine cotton machine-embroidery thread. The weight is similar to these fabrics and it will make smooth seams, especially when combined with a short stitch length.

Stitching straight seams through elastic can stretch it out of shape. The problem is those knots again; they take up more room than just thread would. That's why elastic is chain-stitched in ready-to-wear garments; there's no knot to displace the elastic. Today there are specially-made elastics (available from Clotilde's, 1909 S.W. First Ave., Fort Lauderdale, FL 33315-2100, 305-761-8655) with channels between the elasticized rows for machine-stitching with a traditional sewing machine without stretching. If you can't find this elastic, use a zigzag stitch to spread the knot pattern and prevent stretching.

Bias or knit seams always seem to pucker, but the true problem is not puckering, it's stretching fabric. When the seam is sewn it's lying flat in the machine. As soon as the garment is hung, the bias or knit drapes and the seam does not. To prevent this problem use a baby zigzag stitch. This is a width 1, length 1½ (20 stitches per inch), normal zigzag. This stitch will give and drape with the rest of the garment for a soft, smooth seam. This also works well on very long seams like princess seams on floor-length dresses.

The quality of your stitching can be improved by beginning your seams meticulously. Hold onto the two thread ends as you begin a seam. Gentle pressure toward the back will help you start without a pucker. It's important to press gradually on the foot control; starting too fast is like skidding tires on the pavement. The feed dogs can't get a grip on the fabric and the bottom layer becomes distorted. □

*Gale Grigg Hazen runs a sewing school in Saratoga, CA. She's the author of* Owner's Guide to Sewing Machines, Sergers, and Knitting Machines, *Chilton, 1989.*

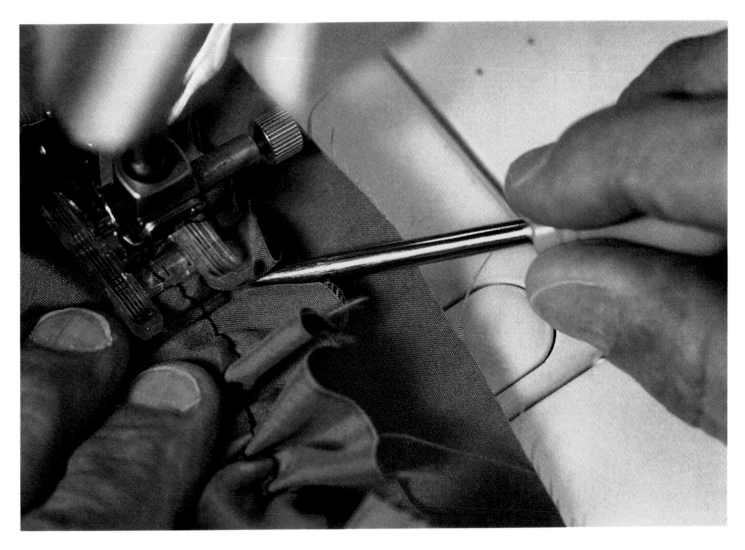

# The Point of an Awl

## This simple tool can improve your grip on all your machine sewing

*by Elissa Meyrich*

**i**f you spend much time working around garment industry samplemakers, as I do, you quickly realize that you can learn a lot by watching these master seamstresses. Almost every samplemaker I've watched at work keeps a short, sturdy pointed awl, like those in the photo on p. 20, within easy reach at all times, and usually has it in her hand whenever she's guiding fabric through her machine.

The reason? Maximum control of the fabric as it goes into and under the presser foot. The awl acts like a pin to hold fabric in place, but you can move it to exactly where it's needed. Since I've included an awl or two in my tool kit, I've learned that there's almost no machine stitching situation that I can't get a better grip on when I have an awl in one hand instead of using just my fingers to guide and

*With a narrow, pointed awl, you can hold a gathered seamline on the stitching line, while keeping the folds in place all the way up to the needle. And with a few awl strokes parallel to the gathers, you can neaten and arrange the gathers much more easily than with your fingers.*

*Keys to greater control of your sewing: Your choice of a variety of sewing awls. From left to right, a pointed awl from Clover; an ordinary seam ripper (use the longer point); a dollmakers' needle; and a thick, strong awl with a blunt tip from Dritz—any long, strong needle will work fine, if you find it easy to hold.*

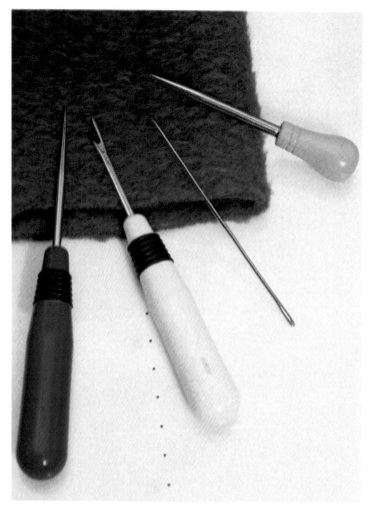

*Stroking the fold with an awl while folding a narrow hem makes quicker, less fussy work of the task than just using your fingers. Tuck under the raw edge by sliding the point of the awl lightly back and forth in the inch or so just before the presser foot.*

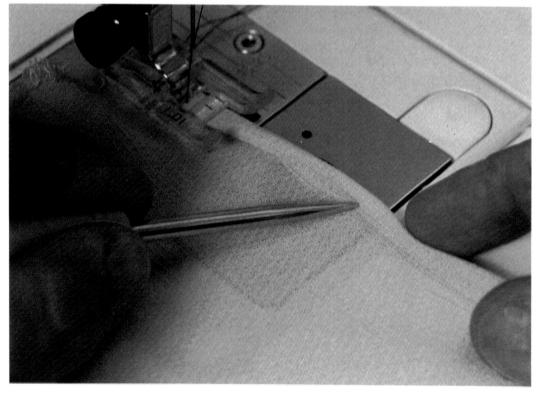

position the fabric layers. The photos on these two pages show some specific examples of ways I use an awl and suggest why one type might be more useful than another for certain purposes. But what is an awl, anyway?

## The original low-tech tool

An awl is nothing more than a stick, even if it is small, made of metal, and sharpened (or rounded) carefully. And like a stick, its most basic use for sewers is simply to extend your reach into areas where you can't, or don't want to, stick your fingers— like between the toes of a presser foot, or even underneath the foot as you're sewing. Because it's smaller and stiffer than your fingertips and usually has a sharp point, an awl can hold fabric more securely and more precisely (exactly between two gathers, for instance) as you press down on it against the bed of the machine. And it allows you to see what you're doing at the same time.

You can buy sewing awls from most mail-order sewing sources (usually for less than $5), but you can also use on-hand things like seam rippers, long, stiff needles, and sturdy pins with much the same results. See "Introducing the trolley needle" on the facing page for yet another option. The chief advantage of a store-bought awl is probably its comfortable, easy-to-grip handle. There are awls available that get progressively thicker towards the handle, used for piercing and forming holes of different sizes in fabric and leather, shaping the eyes of handmade buttonholes, and so on, and they'll work fine for the techniques described here. Awls are also called stilettos or bodkins. By any name, one belongs in your sewing tool kit. □

*Elissa Meyrich teaches sewing in her New York City creative center, Sew Fast, Sew Easy, and at Parsons School of Design.*

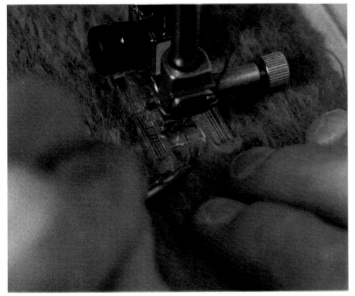

Two layers of heavy coating bow before the firm and precisely placed pressure of a sturdy, blunt-tipped awl, to feed smoothly under the foot. A sharper-pointed awl wouldn't have worked as well under the pressure required, and would have pierced the fabric rather than pushing it.

To ease a deep V neckline to its interfaced and less stretched facing, slip an awl between the layers to control and position the longer, rippling edge, while holding the shorter edge flat. The top layer here is folded back for clarity.

# Introducing the trolley needle

*by Collette Wolff*

A sturdy T-pin has been my indispensible version of a sewing awl for years. It replaces my clumsy fingers with delicate precision, holding layers of piecing together exactly on the seamline all the way through the toes of the presser foot. But recently I've made a discovery that has shaken the T-pin's preeminant role; you can see it in the photo below. It's called a trolley needle. Embroiderers use it to smooth their satin stitches, but to me it's the ultimate finger extension. Once I got used to wearing what could be a lethal weapon on my finger, I relished its advantages. Because it's attached, I don't have to put it down and pick it up all the time. I can't drop it in the middle of a seam or mislay it between seams. Since I don't have to grasp it tightly, I avoid finger cramps. For sewing quantities of quilt patches together, it's ideal. I got mine from Hummingbird House (PO Box 4242, Palm Desert, CA 92261; 619-771-1545) for $6.50 plus $1.50 S&H.

*Colette Wolff is a designer and quilter in New York City.*

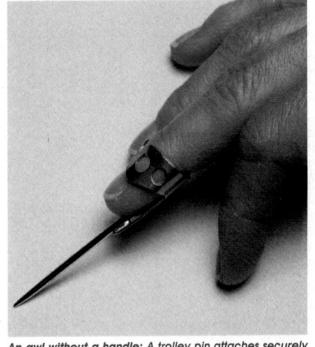

**An awl without a handle:** A trolley pin attaches securely and comfortably to any fingertip, turning it into an easy-to-use awl.

# On Serging Knits

## How to set your thread tensions and match the stitch to your fabric

*by Diana Davies*

everybody knows that sergers are the best tool for the job when you're sewing knits. Their stitches stretch, they're faster than conventional machines, they make the seams look great on the inside, and so on. All of which makes it even more irritating when you can't figure out how to get *your* precious serger to make a seam that doesn't ripple, pull apart, or snap under pressure—the dratted thing is so darn complicated!

It's true that your serger, and the stitches it produces, are considerably more complicated than your regular sewing machine (and how many of us really understand that?), but sergers are certainly not too complex for ordinary mortals to figure out, at least enough to adjust them when necessary. And for good results on any fabric, you *do* need to adjust sergers more often than you would regular machines; it just comes with the territory.

Let's look first at the various components of the two most common serger stitches (the three- and the four-thread overlock) to see how adjusting them affects the serger's performance on any fabric, knit or woven. Then, in "Serging hints for specific knits" on p. 25, we'll examine a range of knit fabrics in light of these variables. The first step is to choose the appropriate stitch for your project.

### Three threads or four?

Most sergers in use today offer the option of choosing a three- or a four-thread overlock stitch. The adjustments described below apply equally to either choice, but for virtually all knits except the most bulky, ravely sweater knits, I choose the three-thread option and save the four-thread stitch for wovens. The fourth thread adds extra width and stiffness along with slightly less stretch and increased security against raveling, and since most knits don't ravel, you don't need it. I sometimes also use a four-thread stitch, set for a narrow stitch width, for ultra-stretchy swim and exercise wear, because the fourth thread helps keep the Lycra yarns from pulling out of the seam allowances. When you're not using the fourth-thread needle, always remove it from the machine.

### Needle threads and looper threads

In the drawing of a three-thread and a four-thread serger stitch on the facing page, notice that some of the threads twist from side to side like ribbon candy, while others run straight along the inside edge, very much like ordinary seamline stitches. These straight-stitch threads (there are two in a four-thread stitch and one in a three-thread stitch) are the needle threads. They're the ones that go

through the fabric, and they hold the seams together.

The looper threads, the ones that weave from side to side, are laid down one on each side of the fabric and twist together at the outer edge of the fabric to cover it. They're held in place on both sides by the needle thread(s), but as you can see in the cross-section drawing on the facing page, the looper thread on the bottom also holds down the needle-thread loops, keeping them from pulling back up to the top.

What I hope you can see here is that, while obviously all these threads work together, it's the needle threads that are the most important. Not only do they hold the fabric layers together, forming the seam, but it's the length (and number) of the loops of needle thread that go to the bottom of the fabric layers and back that determines how much the seam can stretch. The looper threads have plenty of room to stretch, but as soon as that little needle-thread loop is pulled taut, it's ready to break. You adjust the length of that loop by changing the needle-thread tension.

### Adjusting tensions

You can think of the tension mechanisms as controlling how much thread goes into each stitch. If a tension disk is too tight, it doesn't allow as much thread to pass as it would if it were more open, so that thread

From *Threads* magazine (October 1993) 49:58-61

# Balanced overlock stitches

These drawings show properly adjusted serger stitches.

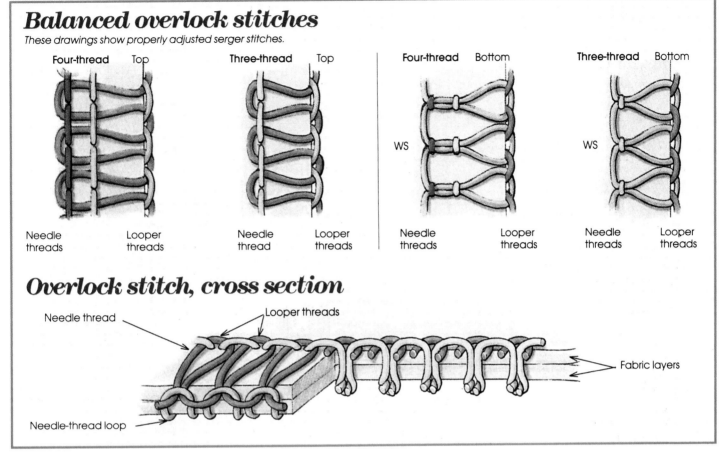

**Four-thread** Top     **Three-thread** Top     **Four-thread** Bottom     **Three-thread** Bottom

Needle threads   Looper threads    Needle thread   Looper threads    WS Needle threads   Looper threads    WS Needle threads   Looper threads

# Overlock stitch, cross section

Needle thread    Looper threads    Fabric layers

Needle-thread loop

---

will be shorter than the others and will pull against them. Each thread has its own tension dial, and on most sergers, the tension is on all the time, even when the presser foot is lifted. Since the needle threads are the most important, it makes sense to balance them first. You'll save yourself a lot of frustration by checking your stitch on a scrap of your project fabric every time you sit down to sew.

**Needle-thread tension**—Needle threads are properly balanced in a serger stitch when the loop that goes through the fabric and around the lower looper thread extends just down to the bottom layer of fabric. It shouldn't be hanging loose beyond the fabric or be pulled tight and out of sight within the layers. (This is different from the lockstitch on a conventional machine, where the bobbin and needle threads should meet out of sight in the middle of the fabric.) Too-tight needle threads break easily, and too-loose ones allow the seam to pull apart, revealing the threads, which also weakens the seam.

There are two rules for adjusting the needle-thread tension:

**1.** Always look at the bottom of the stitch to read the needle tension. Here's what you're looking for: Thread loops, which mean the thread is too loose; dimples in the fabric, which mean it's too tight; or lit-tle dots of just-visible thread, which mean the tension is just right. The top drawing on p. 24 shows examples of the unbalanced effects.

**2.** Since the little dots are hard to see, always start by loosening the tension until you can see loops, then tighten gradually until tension is not too loose anymore.

In a four-thread stitch you've got two needle threads to adjust. Ideally, they'll be the same, but it's hard to be precise. As long as neither thread breaks when the fabric stretches, nor shows loops on the bottom, don't worry about matching.

**Looper-thread tensions**—In addition to holding the needle threads on the bottom, the looper threads keep the fabric

## Serger seam checklist

| | |
|---|---|
| Seams break when stretched | Loosen needle-thread tension, shorten stitch length. |
| Seams pull apart | Tighten needle-thread tension, shorten stitch length. |
| Seams ripple | Lengthen stitch length. Set differential feed to greater than 1. Reduce presser foot pressure. Include stabilizer or elastic in seam. |

edges from raveling, but if they're too loose, the edges can still move and fray, and the loose threads can be easily snagged and broken. If the looper threads are too tight, they stiffen and distort the seam.

When looper thread tensions are *equalized*, they join together right at the edge of the fabric layers, neither pulled to the top nor to the bottom. If the looper tensions as a whole are too tight, they may still be equalized, but the looper threads will be pulling up the fabric edges. If looper threads are too loose, they'll be hanging too far away from the edges, leaving the edges subject to snagging, and will be unsightly if the seam is a decorative one. The looper threads shown in the needle-thread drawings above are all balanced (both equalized and right on the edge), and in the drawings on p. 24 you can see a few off-balance variations.

Start adjusting by equalizing, working on small sample swatches. If the threads need equalizing, loosen the tighter (i.e., shorter) thread, then pull the loops where the looper threads join away from the edge. This makes it easier to see if either thread is still longer than the other. Tighten both threads gradually until they are right on the edge but not pulling it in or distorting it. Sometimes it's easier to feel this than to see it. Gently pull your

# Adjusting needle tensions

*Always check needle tension settings by looking at size of loop on the bottom of your seam.*

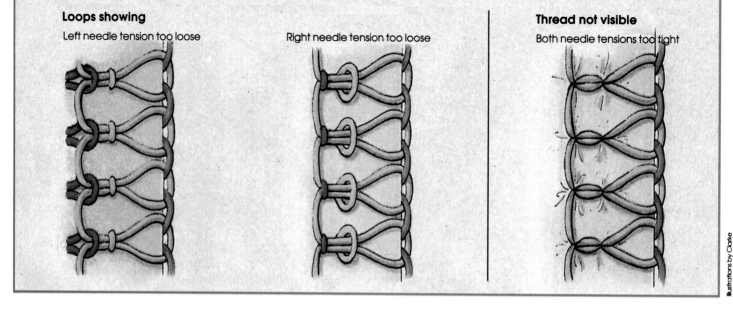

**Loops showing**

Left needle tension too loose

Right needle tension too loose

**Thread not visible**

Both needle tensions too tight

*Illustrations by Clarke*

fingers outwards over the edge of the stitch, feeling for a slight bump or curve in the fabric.

## Matching your stitch to knit fabric

Even if your stitch looks balanced, you may still encounter three typical problems when you're serging knits: seams that ripple because the stitches are too close together (i.e., the stitch length is too short), which stretches the fabric; seams that break when stretched because the needle tensions are too tight or the stitches are too far apart (i.e., stitch length is too long); and seams that pull apart because the needle tensions are too loose. Adjusting to solve one of these problems may create another, so finding the ideal settings is usually a balancing act between the various elements that you can control, including the needle tensions, stitch length, and differential feed settings.

Here's why changing the stitch length can affect the stretch and the rippling: The more times per inch the needle thread goes through the fabric, the more up-and-down loops there will be (see the cross-section drawing on p. 23), so the more thread there will be to stretch out per inch. However, the more thread you add to the fabric per inch, the more the buildup of thread will expand the fabric, causing rippling.

**The procedure for knits**—All this may sound hopelessly complex, but don't panic! The chart on p. 23 outlines what to do for each problem, and there's a simple procedure for checking each one in the

## Unbalanced looper threads

Top looper thread too tight

Top

Needle threads

Bottom

Lower looper thread too tight

proper order that you can use every time you sew.

**1.** Set needle tension(s) that look good, as described above.

**2.** Set the stitch length as short as possible without creating rippling. I usually start at 2 or 2.5 mm depending on the knit. See the facing page for specific recommendations for various knit fabrics.

**3.** Check the stretch by pulling the fabric parallel to the seam. The seam should stretch as much as the rest of the fabric, so the garment can move and drape properly, and so the thread won't break. Loosen the needle tension as necessary to prevent breakage.

**4.** Check the seam by pulling it apart from the right side. You may have to accept the seam pulling apart slightly in order to get sufficient stretch. The shorter the stitch length, the less noticeable this will be.

**Still rippling?**—Spongy knits, such as sweater knits or even some interlocks, can be difficult to keep from rippling, often because they aren't feeding properly. First follow the above procedure to set your stitch. Then try using differential feed (see *Threads* No. 49, p. 18) if you have it, with a setting greater than 1. Because this eases more fabric into each stitch than if the feed is set to 1, it has the same effect as lengthening the stitch. Check your stretch when you increase the setting. If you don't have differential feed, you can get a similar effect by holding your finger on the fabric just behind the presser foot, so the fabric scrunches up, slowing down as it gets stitched.

Loosening the presser foot pressure will also make bulky, spongy fabrics feed more readily. This, too, has the effect of lengthening the stitch, so check the stretch if you try this. The consolation is that most of these bulky fabrics will hide a seam that pulls apart slightly, so looser needle tensions are not a problem. If all else fails, you can feed some clear elastic into the seam to control rippling while providing stretch. Use an accessory elastic foot if you like to tension the elastic evenly, and sew some samples to set the tension clamp on the elastic foot properly. Make sure the needle(s) actually go through the elastic.

## About knits and seams

The problems I've been describing with knits arise chiefly because of the stretch inherent in knit fabrics, and are complicated by the fact that most knits stretch different amounts in different directions. Garments, of course, need various kinds of seams in different places, so matching up these variables is part of the serging-on-knits riddle, too.

Most knits are more stretchy in the crosswise direction, and you almost always want to have the direction of greatest stretch going horizontally around your body. As a result, the horizontal seams (at hem, wrist, neckline, and shoulder) are subject to more strain and breakage than the vertical seams (at underarm, side, and armhole).

I suggest you set and test your stitches on seams that go both lengthwise and crosswise, and take careful note of which is which. If you can find a stitch setting that works with your fabric in the most stretchy direction, you'll have no trouble in the less stretchy one. Sometimes you'll find that you have to allow a little looseness in your needle tensions for stretchy horizontal seams, which you can remove on the more stable vertical seams.

Fortunately, horizontal seams are often supported on knit garments by ribbing, which has good stretch and excellent recovery (it relaxes back to the same size as before stretching), or are stitched with a blind-hem stitch, which works best when the needle tensions are loosened. Shoulder seams are the chief exception, since you usually don't want them to stretch or sag. You can stitch shoulder seams over a nonstretch stabilizer such as narrow twill tape, or strips of sheer tricot as described above for clear elastic. □

*Diana Davies is a sewing teacher and the author of* Understanding Sergers*, which is available from her at PO Box 26333, Shoreview, MN 55126.*

# Serging hints for specific knits

Here are brief descriptions of the most common categories of knit fabric, along with my recommendations for handling them on your serger. Unless stated otherwise, I'm assuming you're set up for a three-thread stitch.

*Interlock:* Technically a double knit, interlock is smooth on both sides and doesn't curl on the

edges. It has a lot of crosswise stretch and good recovery, so it can be used in place of ribbing. It has a tendency to ripple. Try starting out with a stitch length of 2¾ mm.

*Jersey, or T-shirt knits:* These are single knits, so the front and back aren't identical. The edges curl

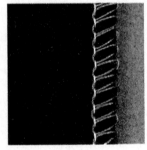

badly, so I suggest folding your yardage in half and serging around the three raw edges before you prewash cotton or blended jerseys. Just cut off the serged edges when laying out. Cut pattern shapes with extra-wide seam allowances and let the serger knives trim away curling seam edges.

Start with a stitch length of 2¼ to 2½ mm, and switch to a narrow four-thread stitch if the fabric is loosely knit and tends to pull out of the seam.

*Spandex:* Also known by the brand name Lycra, spandex is an elastic fiber blended in small amounts with other fibers to create knits that stretch considerably in both directions. Spandex will usually accept a short three- or four-thread stitch length: start around 2. Rippling

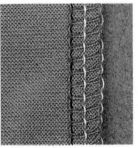

is usually not a problem because of spandex's excellent recovery.

*Nylon tricot:* Typically used for lingerie, tricot almost never ravels, so you can use a very narrow three-thread stitch, and the rolled-edge stitch finger if your machine has one, which will create a narrow stitch. Use a fine needle and

extra-fine lingerie thread if possible. Start with a 1½ mm stitch length. Loosen needle tensions if you get puckers, and control rippling with a differential feed setting above 1.

*Sweater knits:* These look almost like handknits, and because of their bulk, poor recovery, and tendency to ravel, they can be a challenge to sew. Serge around the three raw edges of the yardage, and prewash twice to shrink. Use a maximum width and 3 mm long four-thread stitch, and differential feed settings near 2. Allow extra

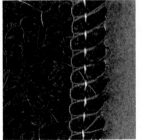

seam allowance width and trim to size as you serge, and support the fabric in front of the machine so it doesn't stretch. Appropriate patterns have few seams, so once you're set up, the garment will go quickly.

*Sweatshirt fleece:* Technically a knit, but not very stretchy. You may have to go up a size and cut necklines bigger if using a pattern intended for regular knits, but you'll have few stitch-setting

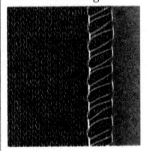

troubles. Start with a medium-width three-thread, and a stitch length around 3 mm. —D. D.

To ensure that the fabric remains flat while you rotary-cut, you can press the fabric to the cutting surface with your fingers just outside the pattern (top inset) or just inside the pattern (center). Another technique is to hold the fabric just behind the cutter (bottom) so the blade won't shift the fabric forward.

# Introducing the Rotary Cutter

## How sewers can use the best tool for cutting out garments

*by David Page Coffin*

From *Threads* magazine (August 1993) 48:40-43

**r**ight after I got my first sewing machine, I bought the best pair of professional, super-sharp shears I could find. Just the other day, I took those shears out of their case to admire them. They're still in perfect condition, and no wonder; I never use them. Since I discovered the rotary cutter, I've used nothing else for cutting garment fabric. From the sheerest silk to the heaviest overcoating, nothing else works as well.

In case you've never seen one, a rotary cutter is a lot like a pizza cutter: a wheel-shaped blade on a handle, that cuts whatever it rolls over. Quilters have taken to rotary cutters en masse because they can easily wheel the razor-sharp blade along templates and straightedges to cut precise geometric shapes.

But if you're a sewer and loyalty to your shears has kept you from trying anything else, consider this: Properly used, rotary cutters are both a lot faster and a lot more accurate for all kinds of cutting. They're faster because rolling the cutter is more like drawing a line than chopping it out with shears, and they're more accurate because the fabric isn't being lifted from the cutting surface as it's being cut. Try trimming 1/16 in. from a cut edge with shears; with the cutter you can do it easily. The cutters are also easier on your hands, and you don't even have to pin down your pattern.

## You'll need a few extras
To use rotary cutters, you'll need some additional equipment—pattern weights to hold patterns in place, a straightedge or two to use as a guide, and a cutting mat. Almost anything you have handy will do for the first two, but you'll need a specialized cutting mat that won't dull the cutter's razor-sharp blade or allow the surface underneath to be damaged.

**Creative pattern weights**—I think it's silly to pay for pattern weights when you probably have some ideal ones around already. I've used everything from my old shears to bean bags, but anything small, flat, and reasonably hefty will do. Any rulers, designers' curves, or straightedges you've accumulated for other purposes are great for holding down long pieces, and you can often simply hold small pieces in place as you cut them.

**Simple edge guides**—Quilters use carefully marked and shaped rulers to reduce their reliance on separate patterns. Sewers, however, don't need anything more than a plain, transparent straightedge to simplify cutting the straight sections of

patterns. I find it useful to have one long one for pant legs and sleeves, plus another easier-to-grab one for short edges. Since I always have a pattern underneath the ruler, any markings on the ruler are extraneous, if not distracting, so the fewer the better. The most important features of any cutting guide are that it resists being nicked or cut by the rotary cutter (eliminating flimsy plastic), and that you can see through it, so you can see where your pattern starts and stops.

**Large cutting mats**—While small mats are suitable for cutting pieces for quilting, you'll need a much larger mat for cutting large pattern pieces. Several sources for big mats are listed on pp. 28-29, but if you can get even a small one now, you can try out anything I suggest here before investing in a larger mat.

## Manipulating the cutter
There's nothing complicated about using rotary cutters, but I've observed first-time users struggling unnecessarily with them, and I've even heard people declare that they can't get them to work. All these difficulties boil down to a few basic how-tos, so let's start from the beginning.

**Safety**—The first thing to do with your new rotary cutter is figure out its strategy for covering the blade when it's not in use. Since it's razor-sharp, it's wise to treat it with caution. Most cutters are well designed for safety, but you shouldn't leave uncovered rotary cutters around where children and other inquisitive folk might pick them up. And don't test the blade with your fingers.

**Adjusting and changing the blade**—While you're examining your cutter, look for the screw knob that all cutters have for removing and changing blades. On some models this is also the knob that controls how easily the blade turns. Roll the cutter over the mat to make sure it rolls easily. Tighten or loosen the knob until you like the way it rolls and the blade isn't loose or wobbly.

**Basic rolling**—As you roll the cutter, keep the blade straight up and down, as you would a bicycle's wheels when you're pedaling straight ahead. Don't bank to the side, even when you're cutting a curve. When the blade is straight, you can look down on it from directly above and see clearly that you're cutting exactly along the edge of a pattern. You're also less likely to stress or nick the blade that way. Rotary blades should be replaced when they get dull or nicked; it's easy to do, but new blades can

cost as much as $5. They will last through many garments if you're careful with them. (Or you can send blades away for sharpening; see *Threads* No. 48, p. 76.) Olfa blades, the most widely available, will fit all cutter brands except Kai/Dritz (see the cutter selection on pp. 28-29).

Now get out some scrap fabric and try cutting a small pattern piece. The main thing is to roll the cutter along in a smooth, continuous line away from yourself while exerting a steady, firm downward pressure. Don't saw back and forth, or move in short bursts.

When you've cut an entire pattern piece, it should lift from the background fabric like a piece from a jigsaw puzzle, but don't yank it away before checking for and clipping any uncut threads, or you'll disturb the rest of the fabric. If you find that small sections of the line aren't cut through, give them another quick touch from the cutting wheel, and press a little harder next time. If there are a few uncut threads regularly spaced 3 to 4 in. apart along the cut, it's likely that your blade is nicked, and should be replaced or sharpened.

> *Properly used, rotary cutters are a lot faster and a lot more accurate than shears.*

## Cutting techniques
You'll probably notice that as you cut, the fabric tends to buckle in front of the blade. This is more of a problem with some fabrics than others, but it's easy to eliminate.

**How to keep the fabric from shifting**—If you're cutting next to a ruler or straightedge, the pressure of the ruler alone is enough to keep the fabric at the cutting line from shifting as you cut. Here's what to do when you're cutting next to a weighted pattern without a guide:

First, don't try to cut through pattern and fabric at the same time. Your rotary cutter can make quick work of trimming pattern pieces, so cut the patterns to exact shapes first and use them as guides.

Now you have several choices for cutting methods as shown on the facing page. One is to hold the fabric down with your fingertips near the edge you're cutting, moving fingers along to stay near the cutter. Another choice is to hold the fabric directly behind the cutter. With

# A guide to rotary cutters and mats for sewing

If you're in the market for a cutter and mat, following are some features to consider. The cutter and mat you select is a highly individual preference, but it's not always easy to try before you buy. In an effort to get a fresh perspective on the current offerings, I asked a group of local sewers who had not previously used rotary cutters to try them and share their impressions.

## Cutter comments

The cutters we examined for safety, comfort, and any obvious highlights are shown on the facing page. Most notions racks include cutters, but you'll also find sources for cutters in *Threads* No. 48, p. 76.

**Safety:** Dropping a cutter or brushing against its razor-sharp blade is always a possibility, so get in the habit of engaging the safety mechanism even when setting the cutter down momentarily. Only the mechanisms of the Quilter's Rule (QR), the Fiskars, and the X-Acto offer complete protection against these likely mishaps.

The QR cutter has the most childproof and goofproof system: a locking shield that takes two hands and a bit of fiddling to deactivate. Next comes the Fiskars, which is the only cutter whose blade,

instead of the safety mechanism, moves in and out of play; the small orange lever flicks the blade forward for action.

Neither the QR nor the Fiskars can be forced to cut with the safety engaged even if pressed hard against a surface. The X-Acto's snap-on cap is in this category, too, but since the cap completely detaches and can thus easily be lost, we deemed it the least safe of all. The Olfa and Salem both have sliding shields that move to cover the blade, but both can be defeated with firm pressure.

The Kai/Dritz has a unique safety shield that is always on, held in place by an adjustable spring, so it's supposed to slide out of the way as you apply pressure to begin cutting. This obviously offers minimal protection, especially to little hands pushing on the shield to explore it.

**Comfort:** If you're cutting small pieces, such as for quilts, you can do a lot of cutting while seated. The manufacturers designed curved-handle cutters for use while seated, claiming that these handles are also more comfortable for those with arthritis, tendonitis, and carpal tunnel syndrome. Everyone will have to make his or her own judgment

about this. The curved cutters require somewhat more pressure, and a different sort of pressure, than the straight ones. The angled-head Salem requires the most off-axis pressure.

Each curved or angled cutter can be set up with the blade mounted on the right or left (good news for lefties), and of course the straight ones merely need to be flipped. The X-Acto is sort of a hybrid—a straight handle that bends at the blade, which is in the center of the cutter, not on the side.

The Fiskars' rounded handle is the most comfortable of all, but users with small hands had to stretch their thumbs to reach the safety lever. The ridges outlining the QR's handle were judged somewhat uncomfortable by almost all of our testers.

**Obvious design flaws or virtues:** The following are more or less subjective reactions noted by us as we tried each cutter: The spring-loaded safety of the Kai/Dritz sometimes interferes with the cutting action by rubbing against and distorting the fabric, despite being adjustable. The Fiskars blade is hard to see from directly above, so it's hard to follow the edge of a pattern unless guided by a ruler. The

adjustable guide arm available for the Olfa is useful if you want to add seam allowances as you cut. (The Kai/Dritz is the only other cutter to offer an accessory guide, but it's not as easy to use.) You can't see the Salem's blade from above while cutting, and its safety lever is a bit close to the blade for comfort. Too bad the X-Acto's cover snaps completely off, since this is otherwise a nice, straightforward design.

## Large cutting mats

For sewers, a mat needs to be at least big enough to accommodate an entire pant leg, and the full width of folded 60-in. fabric, which means the mat should be at least 30 in. wide by 45 in. long. Only two companies that I know of sell mats that big designed for rotary cutters. The Sewing Emporium (PO Box 5049, Chula Vista, CA 92012, 619-420-3490), and the Sew/Fit Company (PO Box 397, Bedford Park, IL 60499, 708-458-5600) both sell mats up to 4 by 8 ft. which can be cut to fit other shapes, either at home or before shipping. The least expensive mat is the Emporium's 30- by 55-in. plain white, nongridded version ($39.95), and the most expensive is Emporium's 4-by 8-ft. gridded one ($142.95). The Sew/Fit

this method you won't have to move the holding-down hand as long as you're cutting in a more or less straight line away from it. When you curve away, hold down from a new position. Start cuts by holding fabric down alongside the cutter, or by cutting the first inch by rolling towards yourself, as you hold the fabric down in front of the cutter.

**Inside corners and curves**—Even when you're comfortable using rotary cutters, it's difficult to tell exactly where the cutting line ends. This makes inside corners hard to cut without overcutting, so I stop short, then clip to the corner with scissors. You can overcut outside corners slightly.

If you find curves a challenge, try a few

practice armscyes, never turning unless you're rolling. For tight curves, the smaller rotary blades are better than the big ones, but you can cut neckline-sized curves with either blade. I'll admit to using scissors on really tiny curves, like on a rounded-point collar, but even these can be rotary-cut with a firm template as a guide.

**Turning the pattern**—When you're cutting pattern pieces smaller than, say, a typical shirt sleeve, you may find it easier first to chop out the pattern roughly with a few quick rotary cuts. Then you can swivel the whole piece around with the pattern still on top, positioning the side you're cutting in the most convenient direction, without disturbing the rest of your pat-

tern layout. This works especially well with small details such as collars and cuffs you haven't weighted down but will simply hold under the pattern as you cut.

## Marking and detailed cutting

Rotary cutters also make quick work of several other cutting tasks in garment construction. I find rotary cutters appropriate for marking match points such as notches, trimming seam allowances, and cutting many copies of the same shape such as cuffs, collars, and pocket flaps with the use of templates.

**Quick match points**—You can make extremely quick and accurate markings on your pattern pieces, especially if you're

mats come in two versions—gridded white, similar to the Emporium's gridded mat, and gridded "pinnable," a translucent, just-barely-push-pinnable surface that has a subtle pebble texture. (You'll find that sheer fabrics will slip under the pressure of the Kai/Dritz safety on the slick, plain white mats, but they're no problem on the pebbled surface.) Sew/Fit mats range from $45.95 for plain white 32 by 55 in. to $119.95 for pinnable 4 by 8 ft.

I've been using the same plain Sewing Emporium mat with an Olfa cutter for over 12 years with no problems. It covers my entire table top, and I occasionally sponge it clean. A wise precaution to take with any kind of mat is not to expose it to hot objects, such as hot cups of tea or irons, and don't leave it in the sun, which buckles it. And be careful not to leave a mat in a hot car or car trunk.

I keep a 15- by 24-in. padded, muslin-covered scrap of plywood near my sewing machine on my mat-covered table, and a scrap of cutting mat near my ironing board at all times so that either workstation can serve for either purpose at all times. June Tailor, Inc. has a cutting-and-pressing product (called The Quilter's Cut'n Press; check your quilting retailer or call 414-644-5288 for local sources) that fills the same bill. It's a 12-in. square

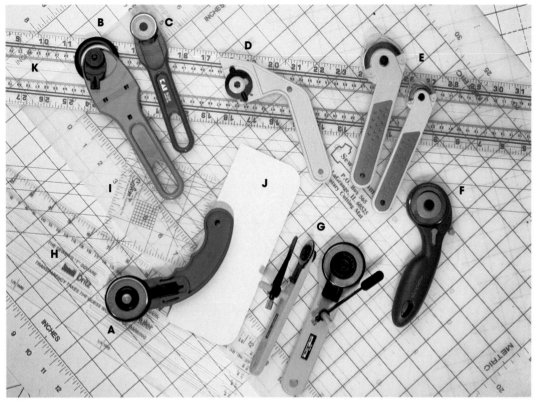

Rotary cutters come with a variety of handle shapes, blade guards, and wheel sizes. Shown here are the blue Quilter's Rule (A), turquoise Kai/Dritz (B), red Kai/Dritz (C), white Salem (D), purple X-Actos (E), gray Fiskars (F), and yellow Olfa (G). Sewers need minimal marking on transparent rulers such as the Scovill Dritz (H) and Salem square (I); white cardboard makes a good cuff template (J). You can make your own cutting edge from a strip of Plexiglas tagged with a transparent ruler tape (K).

cutting mat with a built-in handle, and on the flip side there's a padded, muslin-covered pressing area.

### An inexpensive ruler

Here's a ruler that you can make that works well for garment cutting. If you can find a plastics supplier in your local Yellow Pages that will custom-cut small pieces of Plexiglas, find out how much they'll charge to cut you the exact straightedge you want from $3/16$-in.-thick stock. I've got a 3- by 36-in. piece that my local store would cut today for about $3 (plus a few dollars for polishing the edges). I put a transparent, permanently adhesive measuring tape on both long edges (from Clotilde's Catalog—800-772-2891—cost another $7), and it's the main ruler I need for cutting out garments. With this ruler and the other two smaller rulers that are shown in the photo above, you're ready for rotary cutting.—D.P.C.

---

using moderately deep seam allowances, such as at least $5/8$ in.

To mark the center of any piece you've cut on a fold, just add a notch by trimming a tiny triangle about $1/8$ to $1/4$ in. from the end of the folded edge. For markings along an edge, roll slightly into the seam allowance at a right angle, through fabric and pattern on top of each notch. The resulting slit may be enough of a marker, but if you want it more visible, roll in at a slight angle to the slit, cutting away a tiny triangle about $1/8$ to $1/4$ in. long.

**Trimming seams**—Try a cutter whenever you need to trim a seam allowance precisely (particularly a long one). Use a straightedge, if possible, even on slight curves, by distorting the seam a little and holding it in place with the straightedge as you to roll off the excess. I keep a small cutting mat with my ironing equipment so I can slip it under just-pressed seams for trimming on the ironing board.

**Templates for accurate pieces**—Whenever you come up with a detail that you'll use frequently—a pocket flap, a cuff, or a collar—take a tip from the quilters and make yourself a firm template to use as a cutting guide. I draw the shape I want on quilters' template plastic or poster board (if transparency isn't important), add seam allowances, and cut the template with sharp paper scissors, except for the straight lines; they're better done with a rotary cutter. Transparent templates are helpful when you need to position the shape on a fabric print or pattern.

### Ready to shop for a cutter?

Now that you've read about what you may have been missing, I hope you'll give rotary cutters a try. If you're convinced that the real question about rotary cutters isn't "Should I?", but "Which one?", you'll find a rundown of the options above. □

---

*David Page Coffin is an associate editor of* Threads. *His book* Shirtmaking: Developing Skills for Fine Sewing *and an accompanying video were just published by The Taunton Press; for ordering information, call Customer Service at (800) 888-8286.*

# Looking for Mr. Goodthread

## Matching the thread to the sewing project

*by Gale Grigg Hazen*

*i*n the beginning, before the dawn of synthetics, fabrics were simple, all-natural, and easy to select. And so was thread: you chose cotton unless you were tailoring wool and could afford silk thread. In fact, there weren't any other choices. Sewers got beautiful stitches and seams without puckers.

This charming picture is obviously an oversimplification, but in many ways, it's more true than false. With the polyester revolution of the 1960s, the sewing machine was thrown a double whammy: 90 percent of the fabrics that sewers selected were suddenly no longer all-natural; worse yet, they weren't even woven. The bulletproof polyester double knits of those little-mourned days created an epidemic of thread breakage and ugly seams, and drove American thread manufacturers into a speedy (and, in retrospect, hasty) response. Cotton thread wasn't working, so they retooled their factories to produce polyester thread, and cotton thread for the consumer went the way of the dinosaur.

Many sewers get very satisfactory results with today's "all-purpose" polyester and poly-core threads, and if you're one of them, there's no need to tamper with your success.

But many other sewers today are not getting good results, and even those who are often have trouble as soon as they venture into projects very different from those that they're used to. Typically, they blame their stitching difficulties on their machines or on their sewing technique, when in fact puckered, ugly seams result most frequently from using the wrong thread or the wrong needle-and-thread combination. It's no exaggeration to say that needle and thread are the two most important variables in your sewing, because these are what come into direct contact with your fabric. Happily, they're also the variables that you can most easily change, although your options are much more confusing with thread than with needles.

The simple truth is that sewing machines were designed to sew with cotton thread, and that's still what they do best. Sewing machine dealers invariably demonstrate their machines with cotton thread, because it provides the best stitch quality. The best thread for any sewing project is the thinnest and most flexible one that can take the stresses the fabric and the garment will subject it to, and cotton is the most flexible of all the fibers made into thread. You can prove this to yourself by pinching a loop of various threads; cotton thread, like cotton fabric, will hold the crease most easily.

Nonetheless, cotton isn't always the best choice, because of the wide range of possible fabrics today. Other kinds of threads can work perfectly well in the appropriate situation. Before we explore those situations, let's take a look at what really happens when thread gets machine sewn into fabric, and how the various characteristics of thread can cause it to react.

## When thread meets machine

As I described at greater length in my previous article (see pp. 16-18), thread whips around the sewing machine at an amazing speed. As it hurtles through the machine, thread is jerked at breakneck speeds through holes that impede or guide it on its trip towards the needle. When it gets there, every inch of thread is pulled back and forth through the eye of the needle about 50 times before it comes to rest in a stitch. Frankly, it's a miracle that it doesn't break more often.

**Thickness**—The eye of the needle is the smallest opening a thread must pass through, and the thread must not exceed the diameter of the hole. Fine needles are the best choice for use on thin, fine fabrics, but puckers will occur if the thread can't slide easily through the eye. The eye on any needle smaller than a size 70/10 is too small for typical size 50 American thread; choose a thread designated "Fine" or "Extra Fine" (for sources of all types of thread, see "Options for thread" on p. 33). Conversely, if you use a fine thread in a needle larger than an 80/12, you'll get a lot of thread breakage.

Every time your machine links top and bobbin threads together to form a stitch, a simple knot is created; that's why the stitch that sewing machines make is called a *lockstitch*. A seam is thus a series of knots concealed within the holes the needle creates, and in each project that means thousands of knots. With the right thread, the knots don't cause a

problem, but if the thread's even slightly too thick or too stiff for the fabric, this accumulation of knots can cause puckering. Ready-to-wear often avoids this problem by using a *chainstitch* on seams that won't receive a lot of sideways stress, because in a chainstitch the knots are all on the wrong side of the fabric.

**Surface texture**—Besides its thickness and flexibility, the surface texture of your thread is critical to the way it will react in your machine, and consequently in your sewing. If your thread has prominent slubs, its passage through the needle will cause first fraying and then breaking thread. If it's rough due to fuzz or coarse dyes, it will catch on the needle, and the stitches will pucker. If its thickness is irregular, it will react erratically within the tension mechanisms.

Once you start examining the threads you buy and use for smoothness and consistency, you'll soon develop an eye for their surface characteristics. Unfortunately, the quality of a particular manufacturer's thread is not always the same from year to year, so it pays to check, even on the brands you've had good results with in the past.

### Thread in fabric

Once sewn into a seam, there are two other characteristics that will affect your results with thread: strength and elasticity. Obviously, thread must be strong enough to create lasting seams, but it must not be stronger than the fibers of the fabric. If the thread is considerably stronger than the fabric, it will cause the seams to pull away and fray. It's much better to risk a broken thread than a ripped or pulled fabric.

Stretchiness can be good or bad depending on the project. If a stretchy knit or bias fabric will put a strain on the seams, you'll need thread with enough elasticity not to break during wear. But because sewing machine tension creates drag on the thread as it's being pulled through the machine, thin, soft fabrics will pucker when the stretched thread relaxes. Crisp or heavy fabrics will neutralize this puckering because they are firmer than the pull of the thread. Anytime you're sewing on a soft, light, nonstretch fabric, try to avoid using a thread that stretches.

If you're using a stretchy thread, make sure it doesn't get stretched when you wind bobbins, as it will simply relax and cause puckering once stitched. You can bypass the tension disks for bobbin winding and hold the thread loosely as it winds. In particular, avoid winding bobbins with the thread still threaded through the eye of the needle, as some machine manuals recommend. Some machines can only wind bobbins in this way, which restricts these machines to only the finest quality thread.

### When fiber becomes thread

Don't assume that you should always match the fiber of your thread to the fiber of your fabric. What's most important are the qualities of your fabric—how it handles. These days, manufacturers can make almost any fiber into almost any fabric. Polyesters, for instance, can be made thick, thin, soft, stiff, gauzy, opaque, and so on. Choose a high-quality thread made from a fiber that will provide the needed characteristics for your fabric. I've included my recommendations in the following list of possibilities.

**Cotton**—At its best, cotton thread is smooth, soft, and very flexible. The best varieties are mercerized, which makes them even smoother and more glossy and preshrinks them. Cotton thread has almost no stretch, so it's inappropriate for most stretchy fabrics, but it's my first choice for almost any other garment-making application. It's available in weights for any type of fabric. I use lightweight machine-embroidery cotton thread on all silky fabrics, including silks, microfibers, sueded rayons and silks, and polyesters; and regular-weight cotton for tailoring with woolens. Buttonholes, bar tacks, and other satin-stitched effects all work beautifully when done with cotton thread.

Cotton thread dries out in time and becomes brittle, but moisture can be put back in. Washing cotton clothing keeps thread strong once it's sewn. If you have old cotton thread that breaks frequently, try putting the spools in an open container in the vegetable drawer of your refrigerator. The thread will pick up the surrounding moisture.  ⇨

Before polyester thread was widely available, sewers working on knits were advised to stretch the fabric slightly as they stitched so their cotton-thread stitches would have some give once the fabric relaxed. This works quite well, but it requires some judgement and skill and a high-quality fabric. It may still be worth the effort if your knit fabric is quite stable and your project has lots of topstitching that would look better with the smooth softness of a top-quality cotton thread. Narrow zigzags and stretch stitches in cotton sometimes work well on knits, too.

**Polyester**—The primary reasons for using polyester rather than cotton thread are its strength and its elasticity. I use it in these situations only: in garments made of stretch fabrics; in seams that will receive a lot of stress, like seat seams in pants; whenever I'm sewing real leather or suede; and in projects that will be exposed to the elements, like swim wear and outdoor furniture. Cotton thread will deteriorate when exposed to the chemicals in leather or when left wet for long periods of time.

There are two types of polyester thread available today, *spun* and *long staple*. Spun poly thread is made of short pieces of fiber whipped together in a process similar to making cotton candy. The results are much more likely to be slubby and irregular than long staple polys, which are pulled out in long, continuous strands, similar to filament silk (see

*Threads* No. 39, p. 16), but without the same glossy smoothness. I always choose long staple poly thread, even though it's more expensive. Buying cheap thread is almost always false economy.

Medium-weight and sturdy fabrics of all fibers can often be sewn perfectly well with polyester. But its great strength, its tendency to stretch out in the machine then relax in the fabric, and its relative stiffness and abrasiveness all make it inappropriate for use on soft or light-weight fabric.

**Cotton-wrapped polyester**—By covering polyester filaments with cotton, thread manufacturers hoped to combine the best of both worlds into a true all-purpose thread. Polyester would provide strength and stretch, and cotton would provide a smooth, heat-resistant surface. Regrettably, what we get is often the worst of both worlds: a stretchy thread with an irregular surface. If it's well made, it can serve as a good substitute for an all-polyester thread, especially since it comes in an extra-fine version, unlike polyester. But it's not a substitute for all-cotton.

**Silk**—Filament silk thread naturally combines a smooth luster with elasticity and great strength, and it has the added ability to keep its shape when pressed, which makes it ideal for tailoring wool. Don't use filament silk on lightweight silk fabric—it's too strong and the filaments can actually cut through the fab-

ric. Silk is a good choice for fine knit fabrics, and its slippery surface makes it a joy to hand stitch with; try it the next time you're gathering by hand, and for basting. Unfortunately, some machines don't respond well to its slickness, and it's been all but impossible to buy (see "Options for thread" on the facing page for more on silk thread). It's also extremely expensive and I am usually just as happy with cotton thread.

## Testing thread

One of the difficulties in evaluating thread for a garment is the fact that most of the problems only show up in the completed project. It is the cumulative effect of the wrong thread that shows. As you sew the individual seams they may appear to lie flat, but when you try the garment on, the seams appear puckered and stiff. The fabric will drape and give, but an inappropriate thread will not give with the garment when it is hanging.

Just as you test interfacing before you fuse it onto your project, learn to sew test seams with the needle and thread that you intend to use. Check a variety of threads sewn into the fabric on a strip at least 12 in. long with at least 2 in. between the seams. See how the different threads affect the fabric, and then press the seam and see how that changes the stitching. Try a variety of needle and thread combinations.

Begin by testing for quality in the thread before it is stitched into the garment. Pull and stretch it. How far does it stretch? Does it return to the original length? Does it change shape after pulling? Pinch the thread and pull it between your fingers, as you look at it closely. Is it fuzzy, flaky, smooth, or slick? Does it have slubs or chunks on the outside? Does it have rough or irregular areas? Bend it into a loop and check the flexibility. Does it stay looped or can it be creased on the end?

Obviously, it's nice to find a very close color match in thread, but thread color is much less important than good quality and the right characteristics for your projects. If you're having trouble finding a match, try matching the value rather than the shade. Often a neutral gray of just the right value will blend in perfectly with a variety of dark, pale, or bright colors in the same value. □

*Gale Grigg Hazen is both an experienced sewing machine mechanic and an avid sewer. She is the author of the* Owner's Guide to Sewing Machines, Sergers, and Knitting Machines *(Chilton, 1989) and runs a sewing school in Saratoga, CA.*

# Options for thread

*by David Page Coffin*

The first place to look for an alternative to your fabric store's selection of thread is at sewing machine dealers. They often have high-quality threads that show off the capabilities of their machines.

**Mail-order sources—** I investigated three types of mail-order thread suppliers: Large fabric and sewing stores, catalog sources for tailors and dressmakers, and thread manufacturers or importers. In each category there are more examples than I can possibly list, so the ones mentioned here are representative rather than exhaustive, with the exception of the manufacturers and importers; the two listed below are the only ones I found that sell directly to the public. Check out any tailors' suppliers or specialized fabric stores in your area, as well as the ones listed below.

Catalog descriptions of thread can be very confusing, but they're all trying to describe the same thing: the thread's thickness, plus the number of strands, or plies, that were twisted together to make it, if that's the way that thread was made. In the most frequently used convention, standard home-sewing thread is size 50, and the most desirable number of plies for garmentmaking is three, so a standard cotton thread is called "50/3," or "size 50 3-cord," or something

similar. Smaller sizes are always higher numbers, and the number of plies is given, so a 60/2 is a thinner thread, with only two plies. If the thread is described with some other convention, you simply need to know what the equivalent to a 50/3 is.

Here are the variations I encountered. Size 0 is approximately the same thing as size 50, only a little bigger, and 00 equals a size 60. Silk and silk-substitute threads are usually named with letters: A and O are for hand or machine, and both are equivalents of size 50, A being a little thinner. Topstitching thread is size D, and buttonhole twists are E, F, FF, and FFF. Popular all-purpose threads packaged for home sewers often aren't labeled for size, but they are usually thinner than standard cotton. Metrosene, Gütermann, and Mölnlycke, the most widely sold long-staple poly threads, are all size 60/3; and Coats' Dual Duty Plus, a cotton-wrapped poly, is slightly thinner than size 50 cotton. Dual Duty Extra Fine is slightly thinner than size 60.

**Cotton thread—**The best all-cotton threads for garment sewing are three-ply and mercerized. The most widely sold examples for home use are made by Coats, Mettler, and Zwicky, and all are 50/3s. None of these companies makes a thinner three-ply cotton in colors; most thinner cotton threads sold in fabric stores are the less strong two-ply variety, designed for machine embroidery or for sergers and blindstitch machines. Coats does make

their three-ply cotton in black and white in sizes 40, 50, and 60, available by mail from them in 125- and 300-yd. spools. The tailors' suppliers listed below sell 50/3 mercerized cotton, usually on much bigger spools or tubes, or on cones, for which you need a thread holder—about $5—from the same sources. Most have cotton in 60/3 as well, in many colors.

**Polyester and cotton-wrapped poly—**Among the widely available brands described by size above, only Dual Duty comes in a thread thinner than 60 (Dual Duty Extra Fine), but all come in a topstitching weight. They also come in larger spool sizes than you're likely to find locally, although the bigger the spool, the fewer the available colors. If you're tempted by a polyester thread you don't recognize, make sure it's long staple before you buy, or you're probably asking for trouble. No doubt there are cotton-wrapped threads besides Dual Duty, but no one I called carried any alternatives.

**Silk—**There are a lot of differing opinions about when and if to use silk thread. The manufacturers and importers tend to think you can use it for anything, naturally enough, while most experts and notions buyers are much more cautious. For many years in this country, Belding Corticelli sold a filament machine silk that was so strong and smooth that it could actually cut through lightweight fabrics, so many experts recommended against

silk, except in woolens. It's no longer available, but others are (Kinkame, YLI, and Tire brands are all filament silk), and they are regarded with the same cautions in mind. Maggie Backman imports Tire silk and claims that because it is available in a wider range of thicknesses (the others are all size 50) and is engineered exclusively for machine sewing of garments, Tire can be used where the others can't. She points out that Tire and other silks are widely used to sew garments in Japan. Tailors here also have always used filament silk thread in many weights, and it's still used in the best factories on all weights of wool. It's available from the sources below.

On the other hand, Gütermann has recently introduced a spun-silk thread which they claim answers all the objections to filament silk, because it is softer; Gütermann has been successfully selling spun silks in Europe for nearly a century. It's available in a size 60 for machine and hand sewing, and in a thicker topstitching weight.

The final objection to silk is, of course, the cost—four or five times that of cotton—but few garments would need more than $10 worth of thread. So if the results are substantially better, it would be foolish to scrimp, especially if your fabric is costly. Are the results better? It's a good question. I'd love to hear from anyone with experience on either side of the question, for inclusion in a future article.

*David Page Coffin is an associate editor of* Threads.

---

## Thread sources

### Fabric stores

**Britex Fabrics**
146 Geary St.
San Francisco, CA 94108
(415) 392-2910
*Carries Dual Duty, Gütermann poly, Mettler cotton, and Kinkame silk. $25 minimum purchase.*

**G Street Fabrics (mail order)**
12240 Wilkins Ave.
Rockville, MD 20852
(800) 333-9191

*Carries Zwicky and Mettler cotton; Gütermann, Metrosene, and Mölnlycke polyester; Dual Duty; Kinkame, Gütermann, and a few leftover Belding silks.*

### Tailors' and dressmakers' catalog sources:

*All of these firms carry many cotton, polyester, silk, and Dual Duty options.*

**Atlanta Thread and Supply**
695 Red Oak Rd.
Stockbridge, GA 30281
(800) 847-1001

**Banasch's**
2810 Highland Ave.
Cincinnati, OH 45212
(800) 543-0355

**Greenberg & Hammer**
24 W. 57th St.
New York, NY 10019
(800) 955-5135

**Newark Dressmaker Supply**
PO Box 2448
Lehigh Valley, PA 18001
(215) 837-7500

### Manufacturers and importers

**Coats & Clark Inc.**
PO Drawer 27067
Dept. TM
Greenville, SC 29616
(800) 326-1610

**Things Japanese**
9805 N.E. 116th St.
Kirkland, WA 98034
(206) 821-2287
*Tire silk; send $4 for color card and samples.*

# Meet the Newest Interfacings

## Low-temperature fusibles are the solution for heat-sensitive synthetics

*by Margaret Komives*

SofTouch

**Y**ou'd think that fusible interfacings would be a perfect match for the current crop of fabrics from the chemists' labs—the microfibers, ultralight polyesters, and faux suedes—since fusibles are almost all synthetic, too. And, except for one problem, you'd be right.

The problem is that the heat needed to apply most fusibles is often enough to damage these heat-sensitive fabrics. To deal with this, textile chemists have recently devised new adhesives that work at lower, safer "silk" temperatures, rather than the "wool" setting that earlier fusibles required. These adhesives are applied to lightweight interfacing fabrics that are now becoming available to home sewers. Here's how to select and apply these low-temperature newcomers to your own sewing projects.

### The choices

The chief sources at present for low-temp. fusibles are Dritz Corp. and Handler Textile Corp., known as HTC. Dritz has a new product called Soft'n'Silky, which is described below. HTC has four new interfacings which have been designated Cool Fuse, designed to cover a wide range of temperature-sensitive needs; these are shown in the photos above. Two of the new products are brushed to create a slight loft, for fabrics with texture, such as faux suedes and washed silks. Two are smooth and thin, meant for crisp, smooth-surfaced lightweights like the smooth microfibers and silkies. (Don't hesitate to mix them up; I've had good results with all of these interfacings on many different kinds of fabric.) Within each type, one is stretchy in all directions, or all-bias, and the other provides at least some stability in one or two directions.

**The brushed interfacings**—The two brushed offerings from HTC are Sof-Touch and SofBrush. *SofTouch* is a very lightweight all-nylon nonwoven available in black and white. It's got lengthwise stability so it can be used in facings and anyplace else where nonstretch is needed, like behind pockets and buttonholes.

*SofBrush* is all-polyester, available in

> *. . . get a better bond with all fusibles using white wrapping tissue as a press cloth . . .*

white, ivory, gray, and black. It has a new textile structure called warp insertion, which means that it's a knit fabric with additional yarns inserted in the lengthwise direction. Unlike weft insertions, which look similar but are stable both cross- and lengthwise, the extra yarn doesn't add stability. SofBrush is all-bias, which allows for complete drapability in all directions. It's a good choice for soft tailoring in mid- to heavyweight dress fabrics or lightweight suitings, and it combines equally well with knits or wovens. As with other all-bias interfacings, SofBrush's crosswise grain has the most stretch, so if you want maximum

flexibility in a particular area of the garment—in the collar, for example—cut SofBrush so that the fold is on the crossgrain. Dritz's *Soft'n'Silky* is almost identical to SofBrush; all of the above applies to it, as well.

**The smooth pair**—The nonbrushed low-temp. offerings from HTC are called SofKnit and Touch o' Gold. *SofKnit* is an all-nylon knit structure called tri-dimensional that results in a fabric with true all-bias stretch, unlike regular (tricot) knit interfacings, which are more stable in the lengthwise direction. It's available in white, black, and champagne, and can be used on knits and woven fabrics, allowing complete drapability.

*Touch o' Gold* is a featherweight woven rayon (stretchy only on the bias) available in white, ivory, and black, whose fusible surface is unique. Besides being low-temp., it's also called "gentle-hold" by the manufacturer. Because typical fusing resins often penetrate to the right side of sheer, lightweight fabrics (the technical term is *strike-through*), HTC devised a lighter coating that avoids the problem. It also doesn't stick as firmly, so they dubbed it a hybrid: a fusible/sew-in. If it comes off even partially after cleaning, or if you pull it off on purpose, it can be refused any number of times, and it's a good idea to catch it in the seam allowances so that the stitching holds it permanently in place. I've found Touch o' Gold to fuse quite solidly, using the method described on the facing page, if it is laundered gently.

From *Threads* magazine (February 1993) 45:56-57

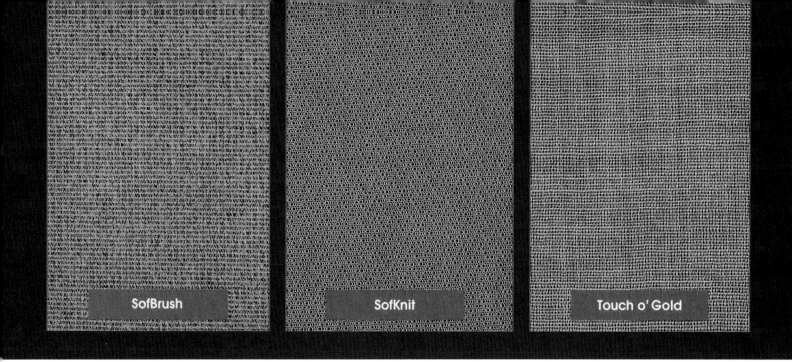
SofBrush

SofKnit

Touch o' Gold

## Testing a fusible

All types of fusing require four factors for success: heat, time, moisture, and pressure. Manufacturers' recommendations for low-temp. fusing call for a "silk" heat setting, applied for 10 seconds, with steam and light pressure. Because irons and fabrics differ, testing is a necessity. I like to cut about a 4- by 6-in. swatch of preshrunk fashion fabric and fuse a similar size piece of preshrunk interfacing to it, leaving about an inch of interfacing on the length and width unfused, as I'll explain below. Here's the method I use to fuse:

First, check your fabric for water spotting by sprinkling a scrap and pressing it dry. If it spots, you can try to get a bond with a dry press cloth along with steam from your iron. However, many irons don't steam evenly on the silk setting, requiring you to spray the press cloth.

A practical solution is to use two layers of ordinary white wrapping tissue as a press cloth. I've gotten excellent results, with no water spotting, as long as I'm careful to spray the paper from at least 12 in. away so it's just misted. I've found that I get a better bond with all fusibles using the tissue instead of a cloth, and if the resin strikes through the fusible, it doesn't ruin a good press cloth.

Press firmly for 10 seconds. Don't slide the iron from place to place, but after about 5 seconds, jiggle the iron a bit so the holes in the soleplate don't leave an impression on the fabric. Overlap iron positions if necessary. Allow the project to cool before handling, then turn it over and, using a fabric press cloth, repeat the pressing process from the right side to ensure a smooth, even bond.

*The new low-temp. fusibles for lightweight fabrics come in four variations, providing a choice of texture and stretch or support for most situations. All photos are approximately lifesize, with the lengthwise grain vertical.*

When the interfacing has cooled a bit, check the adhesion by tugging on a corner. Unless the interfacing is Touch o' Gold, it shouldn't pull up. Fold it and feel it. Does it have the characteristics you want it to have? Did any resin strike through? If it did, the interfacing is too heavy. If the fabric is a bit transparent, did the color change? If so, try a more sheer interfacing, or a beige tone. Did the structure of the interfacing show through? If the garment is washable, it's a good idea to put a test sample of interfacing through the same type of laundering procedure the garment will get. Baste the edges if you're using Touch o' Gold, or you may lose the interfacing.

If the bond is not satisfactory, repeat the process, increasing the time, the pressure, the moisture (very cautiously), and, only as a last resort, the heat. When all else fails, try another fusible, or consider using a sew-in. Some fabric finishes resist fusibles of all sorts.

## Preshrinking and laundering

Because the worst problems that fusibles create come from shrinkage, I feel that it's important to preshrink all of them. You can do this without harming the interfacing or the resin by placing the folded piece into hot water and leaving it there until the water has cooled. Place the interfacing on a terry-cloth towel to drain, then spread it out on nylon carpeting so it can dry flat. The hot water will not disturb the resin but agitation can, so be sure to handle the interfacing gently

during the preshrinking process. I preshrink all of my fusibles this way before I store them, so I never have to wonder if I've preshrunk the piece that I'm about to use. Of course, the fashion fabric should be preshrunk before fusing as well.

I leave a little of the fusible unfused in my test because that can help show whether I need to preshrink even further. If there's any rippling or curling of either interfacing or fabric at the fused edge, it's an indication of a slight shrinkage which might not show up if the entire piece was fused. Laundering may result in bubbling, which is another indication of further shrinkage. The shrinkage may be from either the fabric or the interfacing, so you should test both.

For example, rayon and cotton can continue to shrink even after an initial washing. On the other hand, interfacings with a high nylon or polyester content are subject to further shrinkage from heat and often need steam shrinking in addition to immersing them in water as discussed earlier. You can steam shrink right before you fuse, holding the steaming iron about ½ in. above the interfacing with the resin side down against the wrong side of the fabric to which it is to be fused. After the piece seems well-steamed, fuse it onto the fabric starting in the center and working toward the ends, following the fusing directions above. □

*Margaret Komives' book* Ins and Outs of Interfacings—A Complete Guide to Their Selection And Use *is available from her at 11108 N. Lake Shore Dr., Mequon, WI 53092, for $11.95 postpaid.*

# Preparing Fabric for Sewing

## How to find and straighten the grain of woven and knit yardage

*by Shirley L. Smith*

**i**f the fabric you're planning to sew with was woven or knit, it has grainlines. And if you want your project to turn out as well as possible, the first thing you need to do with that fabric is make sure the grains are straight. Checking the grain of new fabric as soon as you get it home gives you the choice of returning it at once if it's flawed, or correcting it before you sew with it. Here's how to tell if your fabric is off grain, and what to do about it if you still want to use it. The drawing on the facing page shows how to locate the various grainlines, and describes how they differ. Let's consider woven fabrics first; I'll come back to knits later.

## Why grain is important

The significance of grain is as simple and fundamental as gravity. If you want your garment to hang smoothly, without wrinkles and distortion, it must be cut so that one of the grainlines hangs vertically, plumb with the center front, the center back, and with the center of the sleeves. In most garments, this vertical grainline is the fabric's lengthwise grain. Garments are sometimes cut with the crosswise grain plumb with the centers to take advantage of a crosswise pattern or design on the fabric. Of course, some garments are cut with the centers on bias, but that's another topic.

In woven fabrics, either grain can work as long as you position it precisely when cutting to parallel the garment centers (and thus the pull of gravity), and as long as the lengthwise and crosswise grains are at exactly right angles to one another to begin with. Cutting exactly on a grainline depends on accuracy when laying out your pattern pieces. To make sure the

*Every sewing project should start out with a layout like this: The woven yardage has been pinned in half, with selvages and crossgrain ends together. If you see wrinkles at the fold, like those you can see here, your fabric is off grain. Read on for your options.*

From *Threads* magazine (April 1993) 46:62-64

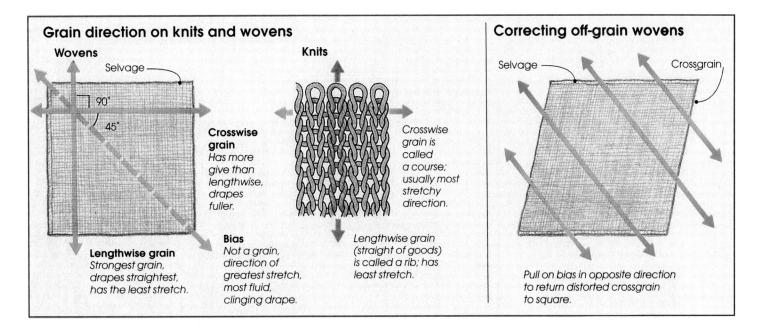

## Grain direction on knits and wovens

**Wovens**

Selvage

90°

45°

**Crosswise grain**
Has more give than lengthwise, drapes fuller.

**Lengthwise grain**
Strongest grain, drapes straightest, has the least stretch.

**Bias**
Not a grain, direction of greatest stretch, most fluid, clinging drape.

**Knits**

Crosswise grain is called a course; usually most stretchy direction.

Lengthwise grain (straight of goods) is called a rib; has least stretch.

## Correcting off-grain wovens

Selvage

Crossgrain

Pull on bias in opposite direction to return distorted crossgrain to square.

---

grainlines are square to each other you may have to manipulate the fabric before cutting. This is what "straightening the grain" means. Both steps are critical for grain-straight garments.

**How fabric gets off grain**
When fabric comes from the loom, the crosswise, or *weft*, threads are at exactly 90 degrees to the lengthwise, or *warp*, threads. In other words, it's grain perfect. But before it gets to the fabric store, all commercial yardage has been rolled back and forth from bolt to bolt for processes such as finishing, printing, and cutting. Each time it's rolled, it stands a chance of being pulled off grain.

If the fabric has a permanent finish applied to it after being pulled off grain, the grains will be permanently locked in the off-grain position, and cannot be straightened. Permanent finish designations include "permanent press," "durable press," "crease resistant," "stain resistant," "water repellent," and "bonded." A permanent finish will usually be noted on the end of the bolt. Temporary finishes, which may be labeled "preshrunk," "shrink resistant," "Sanforized," or "flame retardant," will wash off and won't affect the grain.

**How to check the grain**
The best way to check the grain of a woven fabric is to lay the edges together, selvage to selvage and crossgrain to crossgrain, and see if the fabric lies flat. To make sure you've got the crossgrain, you can pull a thread on one end of the yardage and cut along it or tear the fabric from selvage to selvage. If the fabric has a crosswise woven-in stripe, you can cut along the edge of that stripe. Printed stripes can't be used to verify grain, since the design could easily have been printed when the fabric was off grain. For this initial checking, it's only necessary to establish the crossgrain on one end.

Pin the crossgrain line to itself on the straightened end. Place the yardage on a flat, smooth surface, and pin the selvage edges together. Ideally, your working surface will have a grid pattern on it so you can use it to check straight edges (see "Choosing a grain board on p. 38).

If the yardage lies smoothly on the board with no ripples along the folded edge, the grainlines are straight, and you can now preshrink it. Most fabric will be in this category. But if the fabric has ripples along the fold line, like those in the photo on the facing page, the crossgrain is not

at right angles to the lengthwise grain, and you should straighten it, if possible, before proceeding.

I straighten every length of woven yardage I buy, unless it's so loosely woven or lightweight that the grain shifts just from handling it, as with some chiffons. With these fabrics, you should establish the crossgrain at each end as usual, but you can often correct the grain as you lay the fabric out for cutting, holding it in place with weights, especially if your cutting surface has a straight-line reference.

Sometimes you'll discover that the crossgrain is curved. It's usually possible to correct this kind of distortion by adjusting the fabric as it lies flat, and steaming it.

**Straightening the grain**
If your fabric needs straightening, first unpin and unfold it, then trim the other end along the crossgrain, so you can check both ends after straightening. To return the crossgrain to its original position, simply pull on the bias in the opposite direction of the distortion, as shown in the right-hand drawing above. Start in one corner, grab the selvage in one hand and the raw edge in the other, and stretch them apart on the bias, then move your grip on both

edges down a few inches and stretch again. Repeat across the entire length of the fabric.

Obviously, this stretching can be a challenge with wide or heavy fabric, and you may need a helper, or a bit of ingenuity. I'll sometimes step on one edge to hold it as I pull with both hands on the other. After pulling across the whole thing, realign the edges to check your progress; you may need to do it again or even to stretch a bit in the opposite direction, if you've overdone it. If the fabric seems difficult to straighten, try steaming or dampening it first.

Once the fabric is straight, with no ripples along the fold line and both grainlines parallel with the lines on the board, repin the edges and steam the entire piece. Let the fabric relax flat for at least eight hours. Occasionally a permanent finish will not be reported on the bolt end. If that's the case with your fabric, it will return to its crooked state as it relaxes, and it will be impossible to straighten.

**Last resorts**
So what can you do if you can't straighten the fabric? Return the fabric to the store, or use it knowing the crossgrain lines are not straight. If you cut the garment so the centers are parallel to the

# Choosing a grain board

Whatever tabletop surface you choose for your sewing workspace, make sure it has an overall grid so you've got a clear, reliable, and ever-ready reference for straight lines. You'll find this useful in many ways, but especially during the grain-straightening process, as described in this article. Even those folding cardboard cutting boards can be useful. They're pinnable and easily stored. But if you can leave your area set up permanently, I'd recommend either buying a table-sized, gridded rotary cutting mat, or, if you prefer a padded surface, making one with a checked fabric top.

If you choose the mat, provide yourself with a lot of inexpensive, small weights,

so you can use them liberally, since you can't pin into the mat. I have a large collection of heavy metal nuts (as in "nuts and bolts"), each about an inch wide, which I typically space about 4 to 6 in. apart around paper patterns and the edges of unruly fabric. Even if you don't use the cutters, these mats make good working surfaces. There are several sources for inexpensive gridded mats that will cover up to a 4- by 8-ft. table, and can be easily trimmed to smaller sizes. (Try the Sew/Fit Company, PO Box 565, LaGrange, IL, 60525, 800-547-ISEW; or The Sewing Emporium, PO Box 5049, Chula Vista, CA, 92012, 619-420-3490).

If you'd like a padded, pressable

surface, cover a sheet of ¾-in. exterior plywood (I used a full 4- by 8-ft. sheet supported on a pair of saw horses) with a couple of layers of wool blanket, or with nylon spring-back flannel, the padding used by dry cleaners on their presses, available from tailors' and cleaners' suppliers. You can also contact Covers, Etc., 20970 E. 45th Ave., Denver, CO 80249, 303-371-9436; they sell the padding for $12/yd. plus S&H). For the top, I used a woven-check cotton tablecloth, since it is more substantial than gingham. Staple it carefully to the underside of the board, making sure the stripes are straight and square to one another as you stretch the fabric over the padding. —S.S.

---

lengthwise grain, ignoring the crossgrains, the garment will hang straight, but any visible crossgrain design line will be distorted and will be impossible to match at seams. If the fabric is plain or patterned only lengthwise, you may never notice the imperfection. To cut the off-grain fabric, release the crossgrain ends and pin just the selvages together so there are no ripples along the fold line. After the fabric is preshrunk, cut it as pinned. If you had planned to use the fabric on the bias, return it, because the bias direction only works with grain-straight yardage.

## Preshrinking

I never cut a woven or knit garment without preshrinking the fabric. Even if the fabric doesn't shrink, it will often handle more easily after preshrinking, and if it doesn't launder or clean well, I want to know that before I put a lot of time into it. Hand or machine baste the ends and selvages together to preserve the grain during preshrinking.

However you plan to clean the garment, put the uncut fabric through the same complete process, to avoid an unpleasant surprise the first time you clean the garment. In other words, wash wash-

ables with soap, and dry-clean dry-cleanables, don't just have them steamed. Wetting from the cleaning fluids can cause additional shrinkage.

I've used the tailors' method of shrinking woolens, called London shrinking, which means wrapping the yardage in a damp sheet until it's moist, letting it dry, then pressing it, but I think it's too time-consuming. I prefer to let the cleaner do it.

### Working with knits

The main difference between knits and wovens in terms of grain is that, while cutting on the straight grain is equally important to the drape of the knit or woven garment, the grain in a knit cannot be corrected if it's off. In fact, knit fabric really doesn't have a grain as we know it in wovens. All you can do is locate the *straight of goods* and make sure you're cutting on it. The straight of goods of a knit is the wale or rib running in the lengthwise direction (see the drawing on p. 37).

The crosswise element of knit fabric is called the *course*. Rolling the fabric from bolt to bolt can also distort knits, and if finishing is applied when the fabric is distorted, the distortion could be permanent, so check the relationship of the ribs and courses in the store, especially if there's a crosswise stripe or printed design. But, as with wovens, even badly off-grain knit yardage will hang straight if cut on the straight of goods.

Unlike wovens, which I straighten and baste before preshrinking (so the cleaning doesn't add to the distortion), I establish the grain in knits only after I've preshrunk them, which will relax any distortion that's not permanent. I baste the edges together before preshrinking so that the agitation doesn't distort them further. It is important to wash cotton knits twice to preshrink. After cleaning or washing, release the bastings, then locate a ribline by pinching the fabric, folding it until a rib is par-

allel to the fold. Move your fingers along the ribline, pinning at right angles every 4 to 6 in. Work from the center to each end.

If the layout calls for a single fold and a double layer throughout, pin the ribline at the fold, usually along the center. If you need a single layer of fabric, replace the pins with a thread-tracing through a single layer of the knit along the pinned ribline. If the layout calls for several different folds, pin a ribline the length needed for each fold as you cut out the pieces.

Gently shake the knit fabric and flip it onto the cutting surface as you would a sheet on a bed to smooth the fabric, then align the pinned ribline with a straight line on the board. If the edges of the fabric want to roll, spray-starch them.

When you've prepared your woven and knit fabric properly ahead of time, your garments won't hang crooked on your body, or shrink when cleaned. And best of all, when you have a burning desire to sew, you can begin your new project at once. □

*Even badly off-grain yardage will hang straight if the garment is cut on the lengthwise grain.*

*Shirley L. Smith is the author of* The Art of Sewing; Basics and Beyond, *available from her at The Sewing Arts, Inc., PO Box 61418, Denver, CO 80220.*

# Sewing Without Pins

## You really can do without them; it just takes practice

*by Carol Adney*

*a* baseball player throws, catches, and hits a ball hundreds of times before playing a game. In sewing, we read, "Sew shoulder seam," and that's our beginning. Practice in sewing to most people means ripping out and trying again.

So I'm about to ask you to cut perfectly good fabric into little practice pieces, many of which you will later throw away. I'm pitching a beginning sewing class that's not just for beginning sewers. It's a series of exercises that I developed so that my students could become skillful, employable sewing-machine operators. But in demonstrating and mastering the exercises, my own sewing became faster, more accurate, and freer from the constraints that were limiting my style.

I've gradually thrown away my sewing pins. I keep one or two around for holding gathering threads, but that's all. What started out as not pinning straight seams has evolved into a sewing method I use constantly. It's the best of two very different approaches to clothing construction: factory sewing, with its emphasis on speed and accuracy in one operation; and home sewing, which requires that one understand all the steps from cutting to finished piece.

There are advantages to sewing without pins. No one in my house steps or sits on pins. I don't break machine needles sewing over them, and my overlock cutter has nev-

er been dulled by one. I recently sewed a satin gown in which every pinhole would have been preserved for centuries.

The most dramatic improvement has been in setting sleeves. After years spent avoiding sleeves altogether, I now look forward to the sleeve with the anticipation of seeing magic happen. The key to this transformation is practice. Rather than wait until I had to sew in a sleeve, sweating over whether I could do this one well, I practiced a simple sleeve until it was no longer difficult, then moved to more difficult sleeves with more fullness and ease.

## Building skills

Here are two exercises I devised to help you get a feel for sewing fabric without pre-pinning. At the risk of sounding schoolmarmish, I urge you to do each of these practices correctly at least six times before you try the sleeve.

If you have some expendable top-weight cotton (or poly/cotton blends) in your fabric collection, here's a good way to use them up. Or buy a couple of yards of fabric from the remnant table. There is no need to prewash before cutting. Cut one yard into 3-in. (crossgrain) by 18-in. (lengthwise grain) pieces.

I use a ½-in. seam allowance in most sewing because it's more efficient. I trim ⅛ in. from the seam allowance of patterns to keep my balance points in correct relation to one another and use ½ in. consistently, except for collars, which is another subject. If you are comfortable with ⅝ in., and your machine has a good mark on the throat plate at that distance from the needle, by all means substitute ⅝ in. where I say ½ in. If you are ready to try something new, find a good ½-in. mark for your seam allowance and try it my way. A wide presser foot and an infinitely adjustable needle make things easy. Simply set the right-hand edge of your foot as your ½-in. guide. If your machine doesn't come so equipped, mark the throat plate with tape, typing correction fluid, or permanent marker so that you have a clearly visible guideline. Since you are training your eyes to work for you, don't use a mechanical or magnetic seam guide.

**Straight stuff**—Place two fabric pieces right sides together with the ends and long cut edges matching (ignore the selvages). Position the pieces to be sewn under the presser foot so that the long edges are exactly on your ½-in. line and the top edges are directly under the needle. Lower the presser foot and sew forward three to five stitches.

Stop your machine and lower your needle to its lowest position in the fabric. Now move your hands toward you to the ends of the pieces, and align the two pieces exactly. Holding the fabric between your thumb and the first finger of your right hand, with your thumb on the bottom, tug the fabric gently toward you, pulling out the whole length of the seam.

If the edges don't magically cooperate in laying themselves out to be joined, adjust them with your left hand until they do, without losing your right-hand grip. If the upper layer moves too far to the right, use the fingers of your left hand on top with the thumb on the bottom to pull the top edge back. If the under-fabric strays, place the fingers of your left hand between the layers, adjust the bottom layer, then hold them both down from the top.

Begin stitching the seam, holding the end in your right hand and the two fabric layers together against the machine bed with the tips of your left-hand fingers. Your left hand should start as far from the needle as your machine table allows, and follow along as the fabric flows under the presser foot. As it approaches the front of the presser foot, move your left hand back toward your right and continue sewing forward. Should the fabric slip out of alignment, correct it as explained above. During the whole stitching operation, concentrate on two things: keeping the fabric edges exactly even and keeping those even edges exactly on your ½-in. guideline. Don't worry about backstitching at this point. Remember, this is only practice.

Check your work in two ways: First, look at your fabric edges. They should be perfectly matched. Any error of more than 1/16 in. should be redone. Second, place a straight-edge along your stitching line. Once again, look for no more than a 1/16-in. deviation from the straight line. Each error here is doubled in the finished seam and multiplied by the number of seams in the garment. A 1/8-in. difference in each seam can mean a 1-in. difference in a four-seam garment.

**Following curves** – Of course garments aren't made up of straight lines only. To build your skill at sewing evenly along curved edges, try this exercise. Cut twelve 8-in. diameter circles of fabric. The goal is to sew two circles together, one on top of the other, in a continuous seam with the edges evenly matched and your seam allowance consistently ½ in.

To rotate the fabric, anchor the center of the circle by pressing down onto the machine table with the index finger of your left hand and "walking" the fabric around with the other fingers. Keep your eye on the front of the presser-foot toe.

**Easing on down** – Now that you can follow a curve and sew a perfectly straight seam without pins, let's add a little more challenge. Pattern pieces are often marked "ease" from one point to another. The two pieces being joined are not the same size, but need to come out even anyway. Easing is simple if you control the fabric yourself and feed it to your machine so that the machine can do the work. It's much simpler than pulling up gathering stitches.

Trim ½ in. from the end of one of your practice pieces. Lay an untrimmed piece right side up on your machine table and the shorter piece right side down on top of it. The first rule is: The longer piece must always be on the bottom. Begin as in the first exercise, lining up the top edges and those to be seamed together, and sew a few stitches to hold them.

Move your hands toward you and match the opposite ends. In the bottom fabric, you'll find considerable slack, which will be eased into the seam.

The trick here is to let the feed dog of your machine do the work while you guide the fabric and nudge it into position. Hold back very slightly on the top fabric, while letting the feed dog pull the excess bottom fabric along. I lengthen my stitch a little to increase the throw of the feed dog. This will cause it to pull in more fabric with each stitch.

Hold the two pieces of fabric in your right hand, guiding from slightly above the level of your machine bed so that the lower piece won't bind on the machine. Use your left hand between the pieces to keep the edges even and to push the lower fabric gently toward the feed dog, as shown in the photo on the previous page. Stitch the entire seam, trying to ease evenly throughout the length. At first, you may find that you have an unwelcome amount left at the end of the seam, but practice will show you how much to pull the top layer and push the bottom so the pieces ease evenly from beginning to end.

Check your completed seam to make sure that the edges are even and that the stitching is ½ in. from the edge all along the seam. Once you can get consistent results with a ½-in. difference in the lengths, try cutting off more in ¼-in. increments to see how much you can ease in neatly. Easing one inch over 18 in. is not too difficult, with practice. See how far you can go before

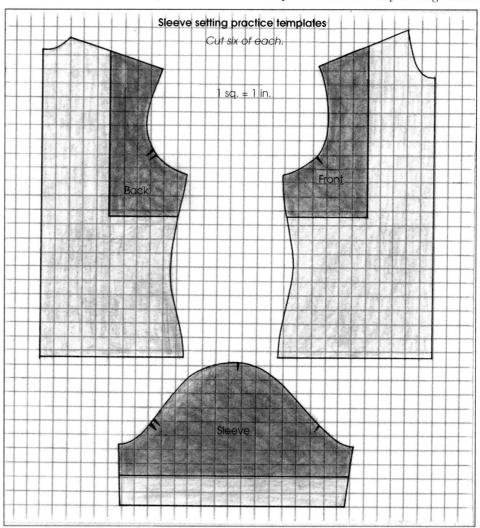

Sleeve setting practice templates

*Cut six of each.*

1 sq. = 1 in.

Back

Front

Sleeve

it becomes impossible.

For comparison, try the same exercise, but cut the pieces on the crossgrain. You'll find a marked difference in the handling, and the easing will be much less difficult. Bias edges are simpler yet.

Easing gives a contour to what started out as two straight lines. This is the most important use of easing in garment construction: it molds and shapes the garment to our bodies.

## Setting sleeves

To set sleeves without pins and pain, practice is absolutely crucial. Cut some practice pieces and sew a few sleeves: at least three left and three right.

You won't need to make three whole blouses, or even one. Instead, make a set of templates from a favorite pattern with a set-in sleeve which needs some easing. Or use the grid to enlarge the templates in the drawing on p. 40. Don't use a man's shirt pattern or a sleeve with an almost-flat cap.

Cut the templates from oaktag, tracing the relevant portions of your pattern's front, back, and sleeve. Cut six practice sets, laying the templates carefully on the fabric grainlines and cutting with a rotary cutter if possible. Accuracy in cutting will make all the difference between loving and hating sleeves. Make sure you have both left and right bodice and sleeve parts. Make ¼-in. clips at the balance points: one clip on each garment front; two clips for each garment back; and corresponding clips on the sleeve to mark the back, front, and shoulder seam.

Sew all the shoulder seams of the garment pieces. Don't press the seams open. The seam allowance will be turned toward the front when the sleeve is set.

Now for the fun part: Lay one sleeve on your machine bed, right side up. Lay one of your prepared garment sections on it, right side down. Make sure that the single and double notches of sleeve and garment match. If they don't, you'll set a left sleeve in a right armscye, or vice versa.

Line up the sleeve seam from the underarm to the notch. Put it under your presser foot and fasten the beginning of the seam with a backstitch, then stop with your needle lowered. This curve should match exactly without easing, so use your seaming techniques to align the fabric edges and stitch without easing from underarm to first notch, following the curve carefully and keeping the edges on your seam guide.

At the notch, stop your machine and lower the needle into the fabric. Lift the presser foot and pivot the garment to the left so that the shoulder seam falls a little to the right of the needle (drawing a, right). Letting the needle and the presser foot

hold the sewn portion, match the shoulder seam to the shoulder notch of the sleeve and hold them together firmly with the thumb and first finger of your right hand. Turn the shoulder-seam allowance toward the single-notched front side of the garment, and hold it in place with your right hand. Don't change this grip until you've sewn the first half of the seam. Place your left hand between the layers of fabric as shown in the photo at right, and, spreading your fingers to cover the distance between the presser foot and your right hand, gently pull the sleeve fabric to the left until the garment and sleeve edges are even. Making sure that you lead the fabric into the needle from slightly to the right of center, sew this seam leaving your hands in position.

Stop as close to the shoulder seam as possible, and lower your needle. Lift the presser foot and once again pivot the fabric so you can control it from slightly to the right of the needle (drawing b, right). Move your right hand to the remaining notch; match and hold sleeve and garment while using your left hand to ease the seam (drawing c, right). Stitch to the notch, lower your needle, align the remaining seam, and stitch even to the underarm (drawing d).

Remove your work from the machine and check your sleeve. Are the fabric edges even throughout the seam? Did you maintain an even ½-in. seam allowance? Turn the piece right side out. Is the sleeve set cleanly, without pleats or puckers? Practice six times, and you should note a marked improvement.

I use this method for all sleeves now, including the puffy, full ones I put on my daughter's dresses. For those, I run three lines of gathering stitches (sleeve right side up, loose thread tension) ⅛ in. apart, in the seam allowance. Before starting the sleeve set, I draw up the gathering threads until the sleeve edge is the appropriate length from notch to shoulder seam, and anchor the gathering threads with those few pins I mentioned earlier. I stitch even to the first notch, match shoulder seam and notch, then use a seam ripper to adjust the gathers in the sleeve between the presser foot and the notch held in my right hand.

I stitch the first half of the sleeve seam, pivot, and reposition my hands. I can then adjust the gathering threads, if necessary, and the gathers. Easing with my left hand, I sew the second half of the seam, stitching even from notch to underarm.

I have yet to meet a sleeve I can't set using this method. From the flattest to the fullest, they go in like magic. □

---

*Carol Adney taught clothing construction and designed activewear before joining* Threads *as assistant editor.*

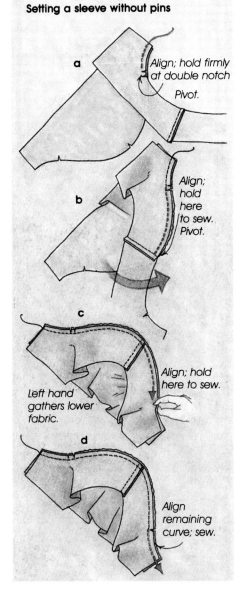

a    Align; hold firmly at double notch
Pivot.

b    Align; hold here to sew. Pivot.

c    Align; hold here to sew.
Left hand gathers lower fabric.

d    Align remaining curve; sew.

*To set a sleeve without pinning or gathering, train your hands and eyes to hold and lead the fabric layers into the needle. Line up critical match points and edges before you start stitching; stop to adjust, with the needle down, at each notch and at the shoulder seam. The fingers of the left hand are spread to control the longer piece of fabric, which is on the bottom. (Photos by Susan Kahn)*

# Changing Seam Allowances

## The ideal width depends on the shape and the location

*by Linda Faiola*

many commercial patterns give sewers the impression that a ⅝-in.-wide seam allowance will produce the best results in every part of a garment. But as a pattern-maker and frequent sewer, I've found many instances where the ⅝-in. seam allowance is simply not the best choice: A narrow allowance works better for some seams, and an extra-wide one gives superior results for others.

A simple definition of seam allowance is the amount added to the finished outline of each pattern piece so that the fabric pieces can be sewn together. Or, said differently, it's the space between the stitching line and the cutting line.

To sew with maximum efficiency, I always cut the fabric with the seam allowances adjusted, which I'll describe how to do. Of course, for narrow seam allowances, you could simply cut the pattern as usual and trim the excess after stitching, but that creates an extra step, and certain fabrics are difficult to trim neatly. Imagine trimming exactly ⅜ in. from each edge of a silk charmeuse garment section—messy. In some cases, however, a wide seam allowance makes an accurate fitting impossible to do, such as at a jewel neckline. If you want wider seam allowances, you must correct the pattern in advance. For these reasons, I always adjust my pattern before cutting the fabric.

## Many patterns, many choices

Patterns today range from one-size patterns with seam allowances to multisize patterns without allowances, plus various combinations in between. Without a clear understanding of seam allowances and their function, this variety of pattern types can cause confusion and lead to construction problems.

Of all the pattern types, multisize patterns have the greatest chance of being misunderstood and used incorrectly, because either they indicate cutting lines for several sizes on each pattern piece and do not include the stitching lines, or they indicate multiple stitching lines with no seam allowances. To avoid confusion, always draw stitching lines onto any pattern pieces that don't have these lines printed on the paper.

On patterns that don't include seam allowances, the marked line is the stitching line. You'll need to add a seam allowance to each edge of the pattern with a clear plastic ruler and a pencil. Be careful, though; flimsy tissue patterns tear easily and can be difficult to draw on. If you plan to sew the pattern more than once, I suggest using spray adhesive (preferably outdoors) to attach the pattern tissue to a more stable paper, such as white banner paper (sold by the roll in the wrapping-paper section of large office-supply stores such as Staples). For a pattern you plan to sew only once, you can use a rotary cutter with a built-in measuring device to automatically add the seam allowance as you cut the pattern piece. Whether you add or alter the seam allowances, write the amount of allowance for each seam on the paper pattern piece and refer to it while sewing.

## What's enough seam allowance?

For ease of sewing, make the seam allowances that will be sewn together the same width. It's much easier to match edges exactly than to align seamlines with uneven edges.

Straight seamlines—It's relatively easy to determine the width of seam allowances on straight lines such as side seams, shoulder seams, and center seams. Straight seamlines can have allowances of any width, depending on how you want to finish the raw edges. For example, on an unlined jacket you can finish the seams with one of several techniques: If you want to bind the edges with tape or a fabric strip, or turn them under

*Choose the seam allowance width that works best for the shape, location, and finish of each seam. At bottom right on the facing page, a narrow width works well when overcast and topstitched or on covered curves (top). At center, a moderate width works for a straight seam that's pressed open and overcast. A wide seam allowance (left) can be turned under and whipstitched to the underlining.*

# Altering seam allowance widths for greater efficiency

You can vary the width of the seam allowances in a garment to reduce trimming and speed the construction process. Seams with concave curves require narrow allowances that won't restrict fit or require clipping, while the convex curve of a puffy sleeve can have a wide seam allowance to support the sleeve cap. Faced edges need only a narrow allowance (a wider amount would just be trimmed away). Straight seams can have wider allowances, depending on the seams' location and the method used to finish the raw edges.

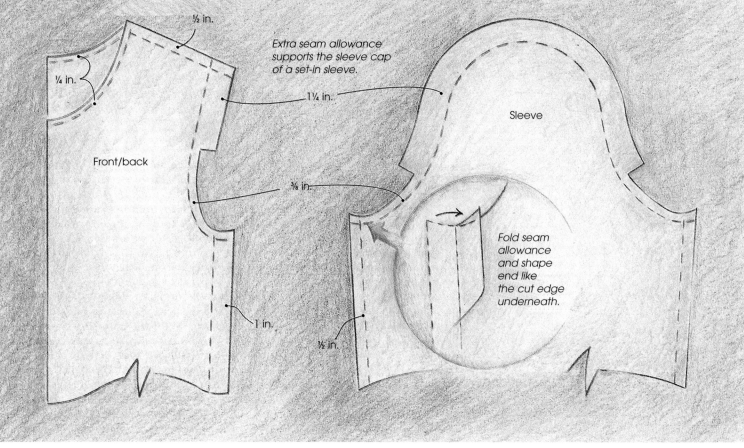

½ in.

¼ in.

Front/back

Extra seam allowance supports the sleeve cap of a set-in sleeve.

1¼ in.

⅜ in.

Sleeve

Fold seam allowance and shape end like the cut edge underneath.

1 in.

½ in.

and sew (as shown at left on p. 42), a 1- or 1¼-in. seam allowance will be easier to finish neatly than a ⅜-in. seam allowance. However, if you decide to straight-stitch a seam, overcast the seam allowances together, then topstitch them to one side, you can accomplish this finish neatly with as little as a ⅜-in. seam allowance.

**Curved seamlines**—A pattern edge can either curve into the pattern piece (concave) or outward (convex). Curved pattern edges need special attention because the cutting line will not be the same length as the stitching line. This can affect the fit of the garment and way the seamline lies.

You'll find concave curves at necklines, armholes, and crotch seams. A concave curved seam cannot be let out if the garment is too small, because the let-out seam will be smaller and tighter. And on this type of seamline, too much seam allowance will interfere with fit. The cutting line is shorter than the seamline, so if you have a wide seam allowance, it will be necessary to clip it so the seam lies flat without binding or giving a false fit. How-

ever, concave curves are usually located at stress points on the garment, and clipping the seam allowance significantly weakens the seam. I recommend using a narrow ¼- to ⅜-in. allowance to eliminate the need for clipping.

Convex curves, such as at the cap of a sleeve and the hip section of a fitted skirt's side seam, have cutting lines that are longer than the stitching lines. These edges do not present the same fitting problems as concave curves, but they may still require clipping to lie flat, if the seam allowance is wide. To avoid clipping, I recommend a ⅜-in. allowance for a convex curve. The cap of a puffy set-in sleeve is one exception, where an unclipped, wide seam allowance will help to support the shape of the sleeve (above).

**Combination seamlines**—For a seamline with both straight and curved sections, such as the crotch seam on a pair of pants, or one that contains both concave and convex curves, such as a set-in sleeve, you can use two different amounts of seam allowance for different sections of one seam, as shown above.

**Extensions of seam allowances**—The shape of the ends, or extensions, of wide seam allowances is particularly important, especially in curved areas such as a crotch seam or the underarm seam of a fitted sleeve (see the drawing at right above). When the seam is stitched and the seam allowances are pressed open or to one side, the extensions need to have the same shape as the areas they overlap. Patterns that are printed with seam allowances already include shaped extensions. To shape the ends of seam allowances you've had to add, fold the paper pattern along the stitching line and cut the end of the seam allowance to match the cut edge of the layer underneath. When it's opened, the seam allowance extension mirrors the shape of the garment cutting line.

**Facings**—Most faced edges require only a ¼-in. seam allowance on both the garment and the facing. A wider allowance would have to be trimmed away before the facing could be turned and pressed, which would waste fabric and time. Edges that will be faced can include straight

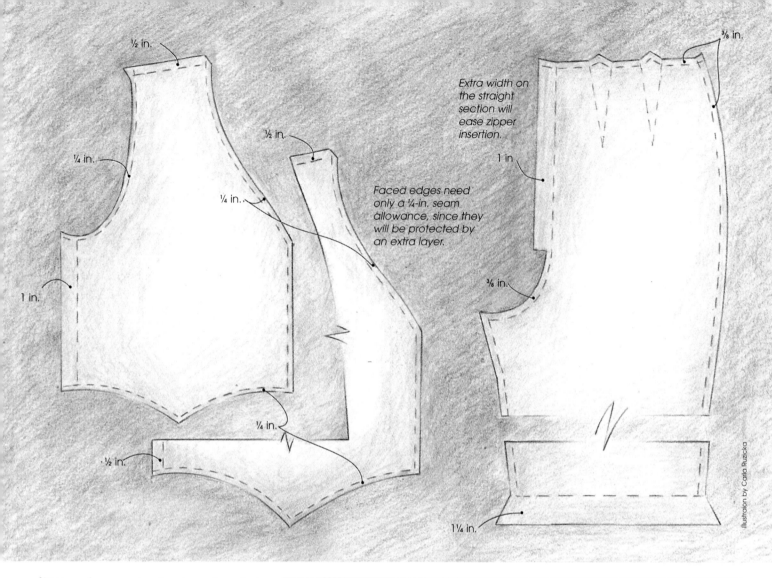

½ in.

¼ in.

1 in.

½ in.

½ in.

¼ in.

¼ in.

¼ in.

**Extra width on the straight section will ease zipper insertion.**

**Faced edges need only a ¼-in. seam allowance, since they will be protected by an extra layer.**

⅜ in.

1 in.

⅜ in.

1¼ in.

Illustration by Carla Ruzicka

lines such as center fronts and pocket flaps, concave lines such as necklines and sleeveless armholes, and convex lines such as the outer edge of a collar.

Even with a tiny ¼-in. seam allowance on facings, you may occasionally need to clip or layer the edges so that the seam lies flat. But certainly this will happen much less frequently than if you used a wider seam allowance.

As you can see, using a variety of useful seam allowance widths can help to make your sewing more efficient. Don't be limited by the instruction guide sheet provided with your pattern; feel free to alter the suggested widths to suit each seam location, its shape, and your sewing needs. A clear understanding of seam allowances helps to put you in charge of your sewing, making you a more efficient and knowledgeable sewer. ☐

*Linda Faiola is a professional pattern-maker who teaches patternmaking, knitting, and quilting at the Cambridge Center for Adult Education in Cambridge, MA. Her article on sewing a melton coat appeared in Threads No. 45, pp. 32-36.*

## *Marking seam allowances*
### *by Gale Grigg Hazen*

I've noticed that the sewers in my classes dutifully draw and adapt each seam allowance to the most efficient width, and then cut out the garment pieces as instructed. But when it comes time to assemble the garment, they frequently forget about the altered seam allowance width and begin to stitch the seams with the usual old ⅝-in. seam allowance (see how well trained we are?), which results in incorrect stitching lines and garments that don't fit.

To help sewers remember how much seam allowance they've planned for each seam of a garment, I developed a simple color marking system to prompt sewers' memories. We place ¾-in. color-coding label dots (available in a box of assorted colors at stationery stores) at each seam on the paper pattern piece. For example, a red dot indicates a ⅝-in. seam allowance, a blue dot is for ¼ in., and green means a 1-in. allowance. I use a yellow dot for hems, writing the amount of the allowance right on the dot. An orange dot indicates something unusual that will need special attention, and I write the necessary information on the dot. Besides being easily recognizable by color, the dots don't tear when I write on them, which often happens with pattern tissue.

During garment assembly, each sewer keeps the marked pattern pieces handy for quick reference. This system helps prevent mistakes and unmatched stitching lines.

*Gale Grigg Hazen owns The Sewing Place in Saratoga, CA, and teaches sewing workshops throughout the country. Her article on ease in garments appears on pp. 46-49.*

# All About Ease

## The amount of extra fullness you need in a garment depends on the drape of the fabric

*by Gale Grigg Hazen*

**Same pattern, different amounts of ease:** *The drapier the fabric, the more ease a garment needs. The two white blouses (sewn from Burda 4463) require quite different amounts of ease to look flattering. The soft rayon jacquard blouse at near right has 15 more inches of ease than the crisp cotton broadcloth shirt on the facing page.*

Photo by Susan Kahn

**S**cenario: You've sewn a perfect crisp linen blouse that you love to wear, so you decide to sew the same pattern again, this time in a beautiful, drapey silk jacquard. The new garment seems, well, skimpy, and in fact you *hate* the way it looks and feels. What went wrong?

Chances are that you've run into an ease problem. Ease is the difference between the measurement of your body and the measurement of the pattern. The amount of ease needed in a garment varies according to style, drape of the fabric, and the way the individual wearer wants the garment to feel and look.

Each pattern is designed for a certain type of fabric (recommended on the pattern envelope) and includes an amount of ease that will work with that fabric. To achieve the same style, with the look and fit shown on the front of the envelope, you must use a similar fabric. If you select fabric with a different drape, you'll need to adjust the pattern for a different amount of ease—more for fluid fabrics, less for firmer ones. Following are some guidelines for measuring pattern ease and instructions on how to adjust it.

## Ease basics

The simple truth is that softer, lighter, more fluid fabrics require more ease to prevent them from looking limp and skimpy, while firmer fabrics need less ease. To avoid a stiff, boxy look, garments made from heavy fabrics should follow the shape of the body with darts, curved seams, pleats, and yokes, as shown in the drawing on p. 48.

You'll find that more patterns these days need to be made up in drapey fabric. The reason is that pattern companies tend to rate the difficulty of a pattern based on the number of pieces it has: A pattern with more pieces takes longer to assemble and so is not considered easy to sew, while a pattern with fewer pieces, that takes less time, *can* be labeled easy to sew. This has led companies to offer patterns that have few but large pieces. These patterns result in garments with little shaping that work best when sewn in relatively soft, fluid fabrics.

Developing a good sense of ease takes some trial and error. I suggest that you follow the fabric guidelines on the pattern envelope, at least the first time you sew the pattern. Then, if you want to use the pattern with a different type of fabric, you'll need to adjust it to allow for the correct amount of ease as I did to make the blouses shown at left. (For information on analyzing your personal ease preference, see p. 49.) Be aware that

# The fabric suggests the style

*For best results, choose a style that suits the drape of the fabric.*

## Thick, firm, or heavy fabrics

*Choose a style that's fitted close to the body to avoid a stiff, boxy effect. Look for darts, yokes, and princess seams.*

## Soft, light, or fluid fabrics

*You can use simple fuller lines with no darts—the fabric molds to the body because it drapes.*

Vest

Skirt

when you change the amount of ease in a pattern, you also begin to change the style of the garment. The fuller of my two blouses resembles a poet's blouse, quite different from the original tailored style.

Besides following the pattern recommendations, it helps to remember how your favorite garments feel, so you can apply this information to your fabric selection. Examine the fabric of your best-loved garments in an area without interfacing or stitching, where you're feeling only one layer. This is the sensation you want to match when you feel fabrics in the store. Many sewers touch fabric on a bolt and expect to feel the stability of a finished garment, so they choose fabrics that are too heavy. If you begin with a fabric that is already the same weight as a completed garment, the result after sewing will be stiff and overconstructed.

## Calculating ease

To understand and experiment with ease in a pattern, you need to know how much ease the designer has included for different areas. This is easy to calculate: Compare the suggested body measurements (listed in a chart at the back of the pattern book or on the pattern envelope back or flap) with the actual finished measurements of the garment. The finished width at the lower edge and the garment length are usually listed on the pattern envelope, and some companies print finished bust and hip measurements on the pattern tissue. If measurements aren't given, measure the pattern, subtracting seam allowances. For each area of the garment, the finished measurement minus the standard body measurement is the amount of ease the designer built into the garment.

Don't forget to adjust the pattern to fit your body measurements, in order to maintain the correct amount of ease. For more on fitting, see "The Right Pattern Size" *(Threads* No. 51, pp. 68-71).

By the way, if you're not within the height range that the pattern companies consider standard (5 ft. 5 or 5 ft. 6 in. for misses), you'll need to adjust the amount of ease, particularly at the hem of dresses and skirts. You will need less ease than the pattern suggests if you're shorter than the standard and more ease if you're taller, to keep the hem width in proportion to your height.

## Adjusting ease

The simplest way to use a fabric you love in an appropriate style is to look for a pattern that recommends your fabric. However, if you have a favorite pattern, you may be able to adjust the style so it works with a fabric that drapes differently.

**Skirts**—To make a skirt with a different type of fabric than the one recommended, leave the waistband as is, and add or subtract ease in the body of the skirt, from the waist to the hem. In a gored skirt, add or subtract panels of fabric to alter the amount of ease. For example, suppose,you have an eight-gore skirt pattern that recommends a medium-weight fabric such as wool jersey. You can make the skirt in a lighter fabric such as rayon challis by increasing the number of gores to 10, then gathering the top of the skirt to fit the waistband.

For other skirt styles, you can add small amounts of ease from the waist to the hem, and then fit the extra fullness into the waistband with pleats or gathers. But if you try to add too much ease, you'll turn a straight skirt into a dirndl, ruining the side shaping and any pockets. In this case, you'd be better off starting with a different style pattern that was designed for your fabric type, as shown on the facing page.

**Pants**—Add or subtract ease for pants in the same way as for a basic skirt. Added ease can extend to the lower leg for a soft, wider leg or taper gently to the ankle.

To accommodate a fabric that has a different drape than what is called for, pants will also need to be adjusted at the crotch: a softer fabric requires a deeper crotch than a firm fabric.

**Blouses**—To add ease to a blouse or bodice, leave the shoulders as they are, and add the ease from the bustline down to the hem, also adding a small amount to the upper-sleeve width. In a blouse that has a yoke, such as the pattern I used for my blouses, it's relatively easy to increase the amount of ease. The pattern I used recommends a light- to medium-weight cotton fabric, such as broadcloth, and includes a small pleat where the body attaches to the yoke.

To use the same pattern with a fluid fabric like a rayon jacquard (or silk, light-weight polyester, or challis), add extra ease in the width of the body pieces, as shown in the drawing at right. To join this new fullness to the original yoke, add pleats or gathers, or increase the depth of any existing pleats. To deepen the upper sleeve slightly as well, add some of the extra ease at the body underarm, and widen the sleeve a corresponding amount. ☐

*Gale Grigg Hazen owns The Sewing Place in Saratoga, CA, and teaches sewing workshops throughout the country. Her article on selecting thread appears on pp. 30-32.*

## Where to add extra ease

*It's easy to alter the amount of ease on a blouse or bodice with a yoke.*

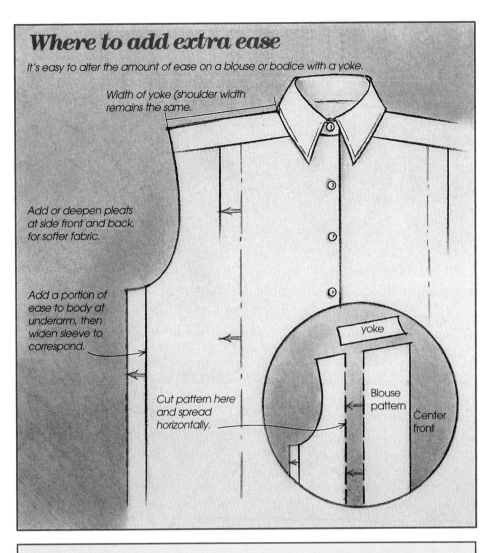

Width of yoke (shoulder width remains the same.

Add or deepen pleats at side front and back, for softer fabric.

Add a portion of ease to body at underarm, then widen sleeve to correspond.

Cut pattern here and spread horizontally.

yoke

Blouse pattern

Center front

## Analyzing your personal ease preference

When you take a look at the amount of ease in a garment, an important factor to consider is your individual preference. There's no *right* way for clothing to feel. Some people prefer the structure of firm fabrics and fitted clothes, while others enjoy a minimum of constriction. For example, if you're accustomed to wearing close-fitting jeans (denim is a firm fabric) and then try on a pair of soft, dressy slacks, the slacks will feel too loose. Yet to hang correctly without wrinkles and pulls, the slacks need the extra ease around the body and the extra crotch depth.

To learn how much ease you prefer, it's helpful to make an ease chart that you can use as a guideline when choosing a pattern. To gather data, measure the bust, hip, upper-arm, and hem width of garments you currently own and like (or go shopping with a tape measure and measure the garments you try on). Then write down these measurements, along with an explanation of the type of fabric and the garment style. Next, subtract your body measurements from these numbers to learn the amount of ease in your favorite garments. This information will indicate how you like your clothes to fit, and you can use this information every time you work with a new pattern. After you've calculated the ease in a new pattern, compare it to similar garments and fabrics on your chart to see if it has the amount of ease you want.

Another way to become more aware of the amount of ease in your favorite clothes is to pinch the sides of each garment evenly, so it fits snug. The amount of fabric in the pinched front and back, on both sides, is the ease in that garment. Seven inches of ease may seem loose, but that is because you are thinking of linear inches. When you pinch seven inches of ease on your body, the result is a 1¾-in. pinch on each side, which is not a large amount of ease. –G.H.

# *Folds in Fabric*

## A turn of the cloth can take more yardage than you think

*by Shirley Smith*

'll bet that the following symptoms have been observed by nearly every sewer: Seams show on the right side of pocket flaps and jacket lapels when they are supposed to lie to the underside. Collars turn up at the corners when they should lie flat. And upper collar neckline seams never seem to end up covering the undercollar seams, even when they've been trimmed, pressed, and rolled on the line that you carefully transferred from pattern to cloth.

If you've experienced any of the above upon finishing a project, relax. You simply need to understand a basic trait of fabric, called turn of the cloth. When you layer two or more fabrics, then seam them together and fold one over the other, as in a typical jacket collar, fold-back cuffs, or lapels, the outer layer has to be bigger than the inner one to completely cover it. Let's take a closer look at where this is most likely to occur and see how to fix it.

### Dealing with roll lines

Because they fold back on themselves at their roll lines, collars and lapels are among the most likely locations for turning troubles.

**Collars**—At the neckline of a typical garment with a fold-over collar, such as a jacket, blouse, or dress, the undercollar is attached to the garment, while the top collar joins the facing or lining at the same point on the inside. The top collar must fit completely over the undercollar, concealing it at every edge, and it must reach over the neckline fold to meet the inside neckline seam with enough seam allowance for the two neckline seams to coincide. On most patterns intended for medium- to heavyweight fabrics, the pat-

tern piece for the top collar will be cut a little bigger than the undercollar piece(s) to allow for the extra width needed. But the exact amount you need can vary considerably depending on the fashion fabric and interfacing you're using. The only way to be completely sure how much you need is to make a quick sample, just like the one shown at top on the facing page.

To make the sample, use scraps of the exact fabrics and interfacing you'll be using for the collar. You'll need pieces 4 to 6 in. long and about the width of the collar, all cut exactly the same size. Interface

## *Collars and lapels are among the most likely locations for turning troubles.*

one layer and stitch the layers together, then grade the seam (trim the under piece to ¼ in. and the upper piece to ⅜ in.). Check that the raw edges on the side opposite the seam are perfectly aligned, and trim them if necessary. Press the sample seam just as you would the one on the collar, i.e., open, then press again so the undercollar does not show on the right side of the sample. It's important to form this edge carefully, as you would on the garment, because the pressed seam takes up a little of the top collar's length just as the fold does, and for the same reason—making the turn uses fabric. You want to be sure your measurement includes this turn, too.

Now simply fold the layers in half, upper piece on the outside, and compare the raw edges, measuring the difference. The amount you measure is the exact amount the upper collar must be cut larger than the undercollar.

Compare the under and upper collar patterns, and if you need to, add to the length and width of the upper piece to match your measurement on your sample, as shown in the drawing on the facing page. If your pattern has only one collar pattern piece, copy it and correct one to reflect the additional width and length you need. I'll describe below how to deal with the excess at the corners as you sew the layers together.

**Lapels**—Once you've checked your collar, the lapels are easy. You just add the same amount you added to the collar to the outer edge of the lapel facing between the bottom of the roll line on the front edge and the collar junction at the top edge. If a bigger upper collar piece came with your pattern, the lapel facing is almost certain to be bigger than the garment by the same amount. You can easily check by laying the facing pattern over the garment pattern. Whatever you find, the difference after correction needs to be the same as at the outer edge of the collar.

To stitch together adjusted layers, either on lapels or collars, pin the layers together with the cut edges even, and ease in the larger upper layer as you sew. This is easiest if you machine stitch with the underlayer up so the feed dog will help to ease in the larger upper layer underneath.

**Lightweight fabrics**—The adjustment for turn of the cloth is slight for lightweight fabrics but still needs to be made. Instead of making a sample or cutting the top piece larger, it's sufficient to merely

*Turn of the cloth in action: These three layers of fabric are exactly the same length, but seaming them together, then pressing and folding the sample as if it were a collar, reveals the dramatic offset of their raw edges on the free end.*

offset the edges of the layer that you want to be the larger, upper one by about $\frac{1}{16}$ in. inside the edges of the underlayer as you prepare to seam them together. Pin or baste to hold the pieces in place as you stitch. This will take care of the turn of cloth at collar, lapel, or similar folds, and will make it easy to press the edge seam out of sight to the underside after turning the piece right side out.

## Handling extra fabric at corners

To make sure that turn of the cloth doesn't distort your collar and corner points, you need to be sure that the upper layer is slightly bigger on both sides of the corner. This keeps the underlayer from pushing the tip away from the garment. The technique just described for lightweight fabrics works well on corners, and the pattern adjustments for heavier fabrics will take care of the extra room needed. But to eliminate the danger of catching a tiny tuck in the larger upper layer as you're stitching around the corner, you can use a time-tested tailoring technique called a *tailors' blister* to help take up the ease.

Before you pin or baste the layers together, fold each upper layer corner in half, right sides together, and slip a pin into the fold, pointing towards the point, as shown at right. Keep the pin about $\frac{1}{2}$ in. from the point and parallel to the fold. Pin right on the fold for medium-weight fabrics and between $\frac{1}{16}$ and $\frac{1}{8}$ in. away from the fold on heavyweights. Align the edges as usual, and remove pins after stitching and before turning. ☐

*Shirley Smith is a nationally known sewing instructor and author. Her video* The Art of Sewing Collars *is available from Sewing Arts, Inc., PO Box 61418, Denver, CO 80206.*

## Adjusting collar and lapels for turn of the cloth

*Add the extra length as measured in your collar sample. Add similarly to a jacket lapel.*

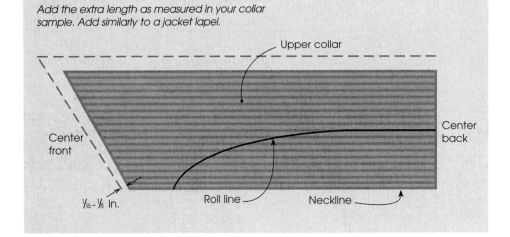

Upper collar

Center front

Center back

$\frac{1}{16} - \frac{1}{8}$ in.

Roll line

Neckline

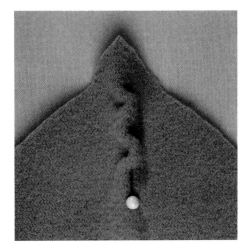

*The tailors' blister: A tiny fold pinned into the corners of a collar's upper layer ensures that the ease there will be safely held out of the seams when the collar is stitched together.*

# *Taming Bias*

## Tips and strategies for handling the unruly off-grain

*by Joyce Gale*

**Growing seams**—*Both sides of this skirt were cut from the same pattern piece, but on the right the seam was cut on the bias. On the left, it's on the straight grain. The bias seamline has grown almost 2 in. compared to its straight-grain mate. The solution is simply to trim off the difference after allowing it to hang out.*

**t**here's a marvelous quality locked up in every woven fabric that only reveals itself when the fabric is cut, folded, or hung on the diagonal, or *bias*. Unique to wovens, bias is the secret behind many garments. But bias is present in even the lowliest poly/cotton, too, and it's often regarded by sewers as a problem to be struggled with when it can't be avoided. Let's take a closer look at bias, not in its glamorous role in couture draping, but as it's encountered in everyday sewing, to see what its properties are and how to handle them to your advantage.

### Bias basics

Bias is that part of any woven fabric that lies diagonally between the straight, or lengthwise, grain and the crossgrain. *True*

*bias* refers only to diagonal lines that are precisely 45 degrees from both the selvage and the crossgrain, as in the drawing on the facing page. This can only occur if the fabric is grain-straight (see the article on pp. 36-38)—that is, if the straight- and crossgrains are exactly at right angles to each other. But any line that isn't strictly on the straight- or crossgrain in any woven is at least partially on the bias, and partakes of the properties of bias.

And what are these? The main characteristic of bias is *stretch*, even on non-elastic fabrics. Because the straight- and crossgrains are parallel to the actual yarns used to weave the fabric, they can be stretched only to the extent that the yarns themselves are stretchy. Not counting fabrics made from elastic yarns, such as crepe-spun or spandex-blended yarns,

the crossgrain is usually slightly more stretchy than the straight grain because the straight grain was under constant tension during the weaving, and so these yarns are stretched out to begin with. But as you move away from the straight- or crossgrains in any diagonal direction, the elasticity of the yarn becomes less of a limiting factor in the fabric's stretchiness. On the diagonal, it's the weave (its looseness and structure) and other qualities that the yarn has (its smoothness, for example) that determine stretch. Because true bias is the diagonal that is the farthest in either direction from being parallel to the yarns, this is the direction that has the maximum stretch that the weave will allow.

Fabrics that are particularly stretchy on the bias include chiffons, georgettes,

**Shifting hemlines—***Here the bias sections of this circle skirt are on both sides of center front. These sections have stretched almost 3 in., and the right side has stretched more than the left. After allowing the skirt to hang unhemmed, trim the hem straight, but expect further stretching in subsequent cleanings.*

**Soft, round folds—***Bias-cut folded edges (bottom) are soft and bend smoothly, ideal for soft collars and cuffs, but the edges will stretch if pressed. Straight- or crossgrain folds (top) form corners when bent, but press into sharp creases without stretching, so they're best for straight garment sections.*

### Locating bias

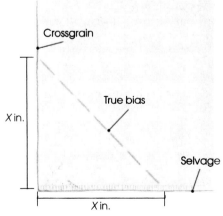

*On grain-straight fabric, measure equal distances from one corner along both selvage and crossgrain, and connect the end points.*

crepe-back satins, batistes, open weaves, and the like. You can judge the degree of stretch by letting the fabric fall from your hand and pulling on it on the diagonal. The less it springs back from being pulled, the more stretchy it will be. Crisp, tightly woven fabrics such as broadcloth, taffeta, corduroy, and so on, will still stretch, but not as much.

Directly related to the fabric's stretchiness is the property of *growing in length.* When a stretchy fabric is cut on the bias, that cut edge will actually increase in length, as if the uncut fabric was bursting with tension that the cutting released. You can see the extent to which this can happen in the photo on the facing page. All fabrics will grow in length if they are hung so the pull of gravity is in the bias direction, but again, the stretchy fabrics

will grow more (left-hand photo above).

When fabric is folded on either the straight- or crossgrain, the fold line, being parallel to approximately half of the yarns, can easily be crisp and definite, because only the remaining yarns are resisting being folded. A fold on the bias isn't parallel to any of the yarns, and so all the yarns are resisting the fold, which makes the fold softer and less well-defined. If you bend these folds, the way you would a fold-over collar around a neck, you'll see that the bias fold remains soft, rounded, and smooth. The on-grain fold will tend to crack and crease, as in the right-hand photo above. If you were now to iron the bias fold into a crease, you'd see that it's difficult to do without stretching the fold, but the on-grain fold will crease without distorting. ⇨

**Every bias has two bias directions**

*Cut symmetrical bias details in the same direction if possible, not as mirror images.*

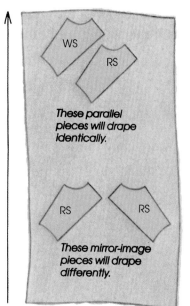

These parallel pieces will drape identically.

These mirror-image pieces will drape differently.

**Bias seams**

*Each bias seam will stretch differently.*

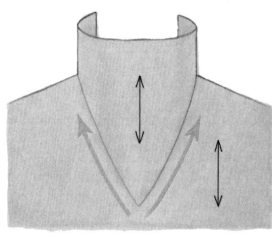

Sew from center to each end to allow each to stretch, then trim off to the pattern dimensions.

**Shift grain to prevent stretching**

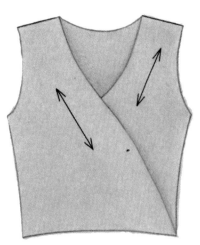

On a surplice top, reposition grain to parallel neckline.

---

At any point on a piece of fabric there are two directions in which true bias exists, at right angles to each other. Because almost no fabric weave has the same number of yarns per inch both lengthwise and crosswise, and because the yarns in fabrics also have directional grains, the two opposite biases almost never behave in exactly the same way on the same piece of fabric. Add this complication to each of the above qualities, and you can see why, among the uninitiated, bias has a reputation for trickiness.

**Dealing with bias**

Obviously, if you want a firm, straight, unstretched crease in your garment, the above discussion tells you to avoid cutting the fold line on the bias. Conversely, if you want a soft, bendable fold, you should cut that fold on the bias and avoid pressing it. And everyone knows that bias binding is cut on the bias so that it's stretchable and can be shaped to cover a variety of curved edges. (You'll find a few techniques for cutting bias strips for garments and quilts at the top of the facing page.) But what other ways are there in everyday sewing to work around, or take advantage of, the properties of bias?

**Stretch and growing pains**—Let's see how we can handle a growing seam or stretching hem. If one of your seamlines

is on the bias and the other isn't, as in the left-hand photo on p. 53, you need to let the bias edge grow before you stitch the two together, or the bias side will pucker from being eased onto the other side. Cut out both pieces the same length to begin with, as on the pattern, then let the bias edge hang for at least two hours so that it is allowed to grow (most fabrics will grow almost all they're going to in a couple of hours). Put the pattern back on the bias-cut piece and trim the longer edge to match the shorter one, then stitch the edges together.

In the case of an uneven hemline, the solution is similar, except that the hem can keep growing through several cleanings, especially where there are no seams nearby to hold it back, even if you let it hang overnight. So I don't bother to hang a hem like this more than the minimum two hours. At least it will be reasonably straight until the first cleaning, when it can be rehemmed if necessary.

**Handling the two different biases**— Take another look at the photo of the circle skirt at left on p. 53. The straight grain is down the center front in the photo, but notice that the stretched bias edge on one side is considerably longer than the one on the other side. This is because of the difference in stretch between the two bias directions.

You can eliminate the difference if your fabric is reversible and lacks a directional pattern. Simply cut symmetrical bias-cut details like collars so that they're cut in the same direction, on the same bias, instead of on the fold, as in the left-hand drawing above. That way they'll drape identically. If you have to cut out your pattern detail mirror-image fashion, you'll probably have to trim the piece that grows longer to match the seam it will attach to.

In the center drawing above, you'll see a situation in which two pieces that are to be sewn together each have two opposite bias edges, even though each piece is cut on the straight grain. When you sew the edges together, it's likely that none of the edges will come out the same length. I'd start sewing at the apex of the V-seamline, and stitch toward the ends, so that I could trim off the end that grows longer. The shorter end will probably still make it past the crossing seamline at the other end. The main point here is that you have to let bias edges do what they want; you can't force them to be a certain length or to grow in the direction you want, because they'll always try to go back to what they wanted to do in the first place, especially if the bias edges will hang vertically in the garment in the direction of gravity.

One way to control stretchy bias edges in seams that won't hang vertically is

**Folding a bias edge for cutting short strips makes cutting easier**

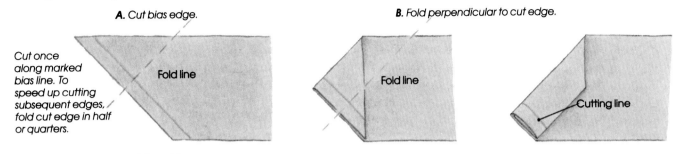

*A. Cut bias edge.*

Cut once along marked bias line. To speed up cutting subsequent edges, fold cut edge in half or quarters.

Fold line

*B. Fold perpendicular to cut edge.*

Fold line

Cutting line

**Making a continuous bias strip**

*Use when seams across the strip aren't a problem. The length of a strip cut this way will almost exactly equal the length of one straight side of the square multiplied by the number of times you could cut a strip that width out of the square on the straight grain.*

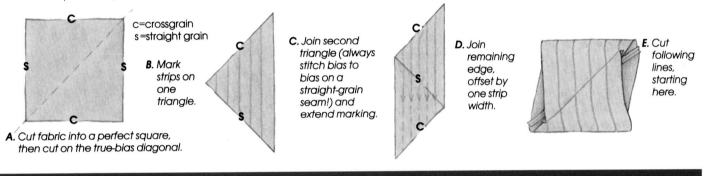

c=crossgrain
s=straight grain

*B. Mark strips on one triangle.*

*C. Join second triangle (always stitch bias to bias on a straight-grain seam!) and extend marking.*

*D. Join remaining edge, offset by one strip width.*

*E. Cut following lines, starting here.*

*A. Cut fabric into a perfect square, then cut on the true-bias diagonal.*

Illustration by Phoebe Gaughan

first to pin the fabric to a piece of paper cut in the pattern shape, then stitch on the bias seamline through fabric and paper. Then remove the paper, leaving the seamline staystitched to the correct length, before attaching the bias edge to the other piece.

**Optimizing folds**—Whenever you want a soft, unpressed folded edge, it should be cut so the fold is on the bias, especially if the fold also needs to bend around a neck or wrist. If that's not possible, consider cutting the interfacing for that piece on the bias. This is what tailors do with their undercollars, to keep even the fairly sharp fold at the neck edge of a tailored collar more smooth and round. Even a small amount of bias can help.

Similarly, ruffles cut on the bias will be softer than if they were cut on grain, and they won't crease as readily. You can take advantage of the stretching that occurs when a bias fold is pressed to create a ruffled edge along a bias hem. And if you make a narrow serged hem stitch over a bias fold, you'll get the same rippled effect, known as a lettuce edge.

## Establishing and cutting bias

The most accurate and safest way to establish bias starts with establishing the crossgrain. Tear the fabric from selvage to selvage to determine the true cross-

grain (unless your fabric has woven crossgrain stripes that you can use to measure from). Then measure equal distances along the selvage and the crossgrain, connecting the end points with a straightedge to make a perfect 45-degree line. Of course, your fabric must be grain-straight first.

The bias is never marked on a pattern piece. *The printed grainline always indicates the straight grain.* If the piece is to be cut on the crossgrain or bias, the pattern outline will be shifted in relation to the straight grainline. If you want to mark a reference line on your pattern when you're planning to rearrange the pattern to place some part on the bias, draw in the exact line you want to make bias, then draw a straight grainline at 45 degrees to that line, and mark the second line the straight grain. If you're making substantial changes to grain direction, and working with stretchy fabric, be aware that the fit of the garment will probably change, too; you'd be best off making a test garment.

You might also want to rearrange your pattern to keep some part of it from falling on the bias. For example, if your garment has a long diagonal edge, like the surplice top in the drawing at right on the facing page, consider cutting the pattern so that the straight grain is parallel to the edge, instead of to center front.

That way the diagonal edge will resist stretching out of shape when it's sewn and as you wear it.

As odd as it may sound, it's sometimes even an advantage to slightly shift garment pieces away from being perfectly on the straight grain. For example, I recently saw a student design project in which a formfitting dress was assembled with long princess seams from top to floor-length hem. Since the dress was made from tightly woven silk taffeta, seam pucker was a problem. It showed up particularly at each long section of seam that was on the straight grain. However, where the seamlines curved even slightly and became bias, the pucker disappeared, because the increased flexibility of the bias was able to absorb the thread buildup that was causing the pucker. By shifting each long panel so that it was slightly off grain, the pucker could have been eliminated even along the straight sections (the fabric was a solid—this wouldn't work with a stripe or plaid). Experimentation would be necessary, but I'm sure the straight grain could have been angled as much as 1 in. for each yard of length without causing more new problems. □

*Joyce Gale teaches design, draping, and patternmaking at Los Angeles Trade-Technical College.*

# Sewing a Perfect Point

## A stitching guide, some turning tools, and a few helpful hints yield accurate corners

*by David Page Coffin*

**Compensate for bias stretching at the point** by shortening the seamline, as shown by the dotted line on the pattern and resulting collar at far left. However, don't blunt the point, as was done for the collar at near left, which resulted in a bulbous shape.

*I* doubt there's a sewer alive who hasn't struggled over forming the points of a collar, the corners of a pocket flap or welt, or the peaks of a lapel. How do you stitch and turn the darn things so the points are points instead of swollen, misshapen eyesores? And how do you get two points to turn out the same shape?

I still agonize a little over each point. Nonetheless, I have had some useful lights go on during my struggles and while watching some skilled sewing professionals go about their work. The critical issues condense to a few important skills: accurate stitching, attention to the trimming of seam allowances, and turning technique. I'll review these issues as I see them and share one professional's approach to turning the corner right side out.

### Controlling the shape with your seamline

As a novice sewer, I was apt to underestimate the instability of fabric, ignoring its tendency to stretch, shift, shrink, and otherwise behave unlike paper or sheet metal as I worked with it. That's why I was so puzzled when, no matter how carefully I'd follow the seamline when I stitched a collar or pocket flap, my turned point still wound up with that familiar bulbous tip and inward-curving sides, which together are often described as a dog ear. This was bad enough, but if at

From *Threads* magazine (June 1994) 53:38-41

the same time I happened to make the slightest error in following that seamline, my error showed up in glaring detail. What infuriating inconsistency!

**Compensating for stretch**—The resolution to my dilemma turned out (in part) to be this: Yes, you do control the final shape of any detail (corner or point or whatever) exactly with your stitching, but you also have to compensate with your stitching for any distortion that is likely to creep into the fabric in the process. As you stitch to and around a point, the most likely distortion you'll create is a slight stretch, particularly if any of the seams are on the bias; the softer the fabric, the worse the problem. That stretching shows up in your point as an inward curve on both sides near the tip, and it makes the tip longer. You can, of course, aggravate the stretch by pushing too hard when you're turning out the point, but we'll get into that later.

The cure? My solution is to shorten the seamline near the tip as shown on the facing page. The best way to know how much to reshape the tip is by stitching a test point in the same fabric—complete with interfacing—and noting the extent of the distortion. Be sure your sample includes at least 3 or 4 in. of seam on each side of the point, unless the point itself isn't that long, so there'll be some seam to stretch.

You may not have to compensate for stretch at all. I've found that I don't need to reshape seams for a firmly woven, stable, shirt-weight cotton or similar fabric, but usually do on softer, looser fabrics such as woolens.

**Stitch a point**—The idea that you should stitch a blunt corner with a stitch or two across the tip, instead of a point, is probably the most oft-repeated advice I've read

To create identical shapes, use a cardboard template. Trace the stitching line and trim the interfacing from the point before stitching (far left). After stitching, trim the seam allowances so they won't overlap when the point is turned (near left).

or heard on how to improve your points. I've decided, after years of doing it both ways, that making a blunt corner is more likely to hurt your results than to help them. In practice, I've found that it's better to reduce the seam allowance bulk as much as possible and stitch the point in exactly the shape you want to see when it's turned. Even in heavy fabrics, I've found that rounding the point can result in a dog ear (see samples on the facing page).

**Use a template for repeatable results**—The best way I've found to ensure that two or more points match is to stitch them as identically as possible. To do that, I create a thin cardboard or heavy paper version of the pattern piece, called a template, as shown above, for the pat-

tern detail I'm turning. If you make the template without seam allowances, you can trace it to mark the exact stitching line on the wrong side of each point. (If possible, I'd use a plain, sharp pencil or a sharpened tailors' chalk for marking a thin, accurate, and washable continuous line.) If your fabric won't take a mark, try stitching next to your template or through a tracing of your seamline on thin paper or tear-away stabilizer.

## Turning tactics

You can spoil even the best-stitched point by using the wrong tool to push it out, or by leaving too much seam allowance bulk in the tip. If you've ever turned a good-looking point into a bulbous one just by pressing it, it's probably because

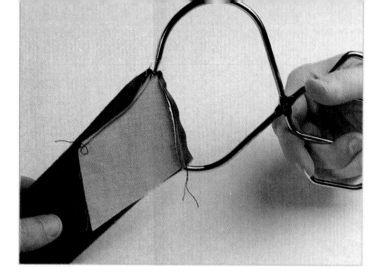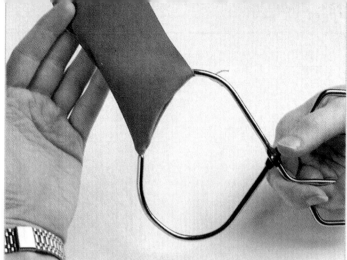

*For a smooth point turn, first pinch only the tip with a collar point and tube turner (left). One tip of this ice-tong-like device is pointed and the other slightly rounded for a clean pinch (right).*

*The narrow surface and tip of a point presser let you press seams all the way to the point without leaving an impression of the seam allowances on the right side. Most point pressers have at least two point shapes for pressing.*

flattening the excessive bulk spread and ruined your tip's lovely profile. Of course, it's essential to press open your seams on a point presser before you turn (lower right photo above).

**Reducing bulk—**Besides the weight of the fabric itself, bulk comes from seam allowances and from interfacing, so it makes sense to eliminate these as much as possible. The easiest way to reduce interfacing bulk is to trim the last $\frac{1}{4}$ or $\frac{1}{8}$ in. of interfacing from the tip before stitching. I'd leave interfacing in the tip only if it was extremely thin and I was hoping it would reinforce a loose or weak fashion fabric against the strain of turning.

The fine points of trimming seam allowances are as follows: Don't trim the tip so closely that you weaken the seam; and trim the sides so they won't overlap when the point is turned, as shown in the photo on p. 57. How close you can safely trim is related to the looseness of the weave of the fabric. Since you'd never need or want to trim closer than $\frac{1}{16}$ in., or farther away than about $\frac{3}{16}$ in., the choices boil down to a scant or generous $\frac{1}{8}$ in.

**Tools of choice—**I distinguish, in my own tool kit, between tools for the first step (turning the bulk of the collar to the right side), and those for the second step (struggling with the final critical tip). The more the first step reduces the work you'll have to do in the second step, the better.

My favorite first-step tool looks like a pair of ice tongs (see the top photos above). It's like having long, tiny fingers that allow you to grab the point, holding it securely and safely as you turn the rest of the piece (the Collar Point and Tube Turner shown is available by mail for $11.25 plus $3.50 S&H from Nancy's Notions, PO Box 683, Beaver Dam, WI 53916-0683; 800-833-0690).

The problem with most turning tools is that they're not pointed or narrow enough to push out the tip without stretching it sideways at the same time (yet another cause for bulbous tips). Of course, if the tool is too sharp, it will poke right through. The tools I use for the second part of turning are an awl or blunt needle and a pair of needle-nose tweezers.

I can use the awl, which is common enough, to work out the point, and I use the tweezers, available at cutlery and beauty supply stores, to counteract the tendency of the point to spread while I'm pushing out or pressing the point (upper photo on the facing page).

My final refinement is simply to hedge my bets a little on the first of any pair of points I'm working on, not trying to make the first look perfect before I work on the second. It's always easier to match a pretty good point than a perfect one. Once they're matched, then I'll gamble on being able to push each one out just a tiny bit more.

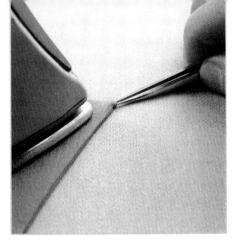

To prevent point spread during pressing, pinch the sides with needle-nose tweezers.

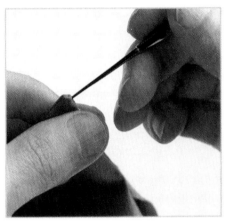

Lift, don't pull, a point outward with the tip of an awl or large needle inserted into the seam near the point to finish turning the collar. The seam allowances have been treated as shown in the drawing sequence at right.

## A custom shirtmaker's method for turning a point

*This method comes from professional seamstress Adriana Lucas in New York City. Start with seam allowances ¼ in. wide, but don't trim them.*

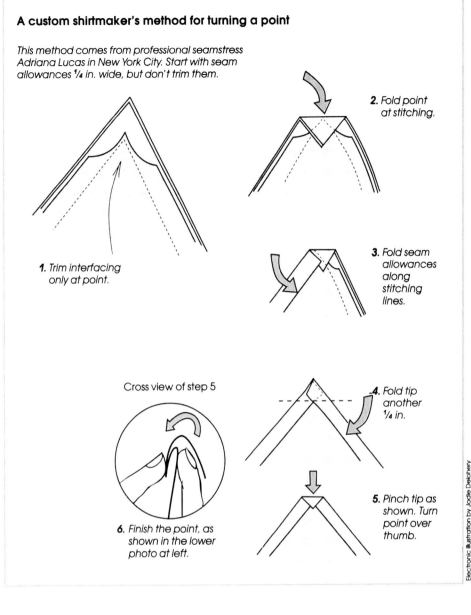

**1.** Trim interfacing only at point.

**2.** Fold point at stitching.

**3.** Fold seam allowances along stitching lines.

**4.** Fold tip another ¼ in.

**5.** Pinch tip as shown. Turn point over thumb.

Cross view of step 5

**6.** Finish the point, as shown in the lower photo at left.

Electronic illustration by Jodie Delohery

## The shirtmakers' point-turning method

There's another approach to point turning that's used with amazing results by custom shirtmakers. It ignores several of the principles (tracing, trimming, using a tube turner) I've covered here, and it takes practice to perfect. It is described step by step in the drawing sequence and lower photo above.

First, stitch the point (no crosswise stitches), then trim just the interfacing, (which was cut just like the collar pieces and stitched as a third layer) from your tip. Finger-press the collar seams open (there's little time for irons in the factory). Then fold the allowances at the tip to the interfacing side as shown in the drawing, carefully arranging the folds so they match the shape of the point. Finger-press the shape for a few seconds.

Fold the entire tip again towards the interfacing, and pinch the fold with thumb and forefinger as you pull the undercol-lar over your thumb. Then push out the tip with your finger as far as you can.

For the tip, insert the point of a thick, sharp needle or awl into the collar seam on one side and under the final fold. Then use the needle point to lift the last bit of unturned point. When executed by an expert, the careful folds that shape the seam allowances are all still in place and the result is bulky (like most manufactured shirt points) but sharp as a tack. The important thing to note is that the tip is pushed upward, not pulled, by the needle or awl tip.

## Maybe you don't need a point

I've come to realize that there is more to a corner than sharp points or the perfect symmetry of paired points. There is the entire contour of an edge or seam to be aware of, and it's entirely up to you how to create it.

Here are a few things to ponder when planning a garment or detail with a cor-ner: Within the limits of your present skills, what's the best shape for this corner? Might it be better with a subtle curve, or perhaps with the corner deliberately blunted with a few well-chosen crosswise stitches? Do the straight seams coming into the corner need some subtle shaping? Or might the whole thing work out better if the angle of the corner was expanded, so the point just wasn't so difficult? It's your garment and your skills on the line, so take your time over the design of the point before you tackle turning it. □

*David Coffin is an associate editor of* Threads *and the author of* Shirtmaking: Developing Skills for Fine Sewing *(The Taunton Press, 1993).*

*Have your own foolproof method for perfecting corners and points? By all means, let us know your solutions by sending a note to* Threads, *PO Box 5506, Newtown, CT 06470-5506.*

# Binding with Bias

Here's a foolproof way
to apply this elegant trim
to necklines and edges

*by Claire B. Shaeffer*

$f$inishing a neckline or any edge with a narrow bias binding adds an elegant detail that gives a garment the look of high-priced ready-to-wear. This binding is cut on the bias so it can be shaped to duplicate the edge it covers, encasing that edge at the seamline and replacing the seam allowance.

A bias binding is as functional as it is handsome. It offers an attractive alternative to unsightly facings on transparent fabrics; tames pleats and gathers that extend to an edge; finishes the edges of bulky fabrics and those whose weave or surface finish makes conventional hemming or facing unattractive; and introduces a nice design detail when cut from a contrasting fabric or color.

If a bias binding is so useful, then why don't sewers use it more often? Usually it's because sewers find that their bias bindings ripple and twist unattractively or appear too wide or uneven in width. These difficulties are due in part to the geometry of a curved binding, where the inner edge is shorter than the outer edge. I'd like to offer a method for successfully binding an edge such as that on a neckline, which will be very visible and must be flawless. The technique that I use is suitable for various fabrics, from fine silks to practical synthetics and microfibers, and for novice to experienced sewers. Although the several rounds of basting and the attention to detail in my directions may sound tedious, trust me; the results are worth it.

## Preparing the garment

The directions given here are for a blouse or bodice design with a center-back opening and can be adapted if your design opens elsewhere. Before working in fashion fabric, make a sample.

On the front and back bodice patterns, trim the seam allowance from the neckline since you'll be binding the edge right at the seamline. If your pattern shows only the cutting line of the seam allowance, not the seamline itself (most multisize patterns don't), you'll need to mark the seamline before you can trim the pattern.

Cut out the bodice front and back and join them at the shoulder seams, then press the seams. Reduce bulk at the neckline by trimming small triangles from the ends of the shoulder seams. Then finish the back opening.

Next, staystitch the neckline to keep it from stretching. If you're working with a fabric that distorts easily, such as a silk or microfiber, first make a paper template (see the drawing on p. 62) so that you can preserve the neckline's original shape as you staystitch. (This is a trick that I learned from Los Angeles designer Michael Novarese.)

With the right side up and your stitch length set to 15 sts/in. (shorter stitches will better shape the neckline's curve), place the bodice on the paper template (if needed) and staystitch around the neckline a scant $\frac{1}{4}$ in.—or the width of the finished binding—from the raw edge. Be careful to stitch evenly since this stitched line will serve as a guide for basting the bias binding to the bodice. Tear away the paper template.

## Construction tips

The finished binding, whose construction is shown in the drawings on p. 53, can be any width from $\frac{1}{8}$ to 1 in. wide, but most designers favor a $\frac{1}{4}$-in.-wide binding. Generally, the wider the binding,

*Getting a bias binding smooth and ripple-free, like on the neck of the blouse shown here, depends first and foremost on cutting the binding fabric on the true bias.*

## *Establishing the true bias*

Crosswise grain

Mark true bias here.

Mark second line at width desired.

Bias strip

Lengthwise grain

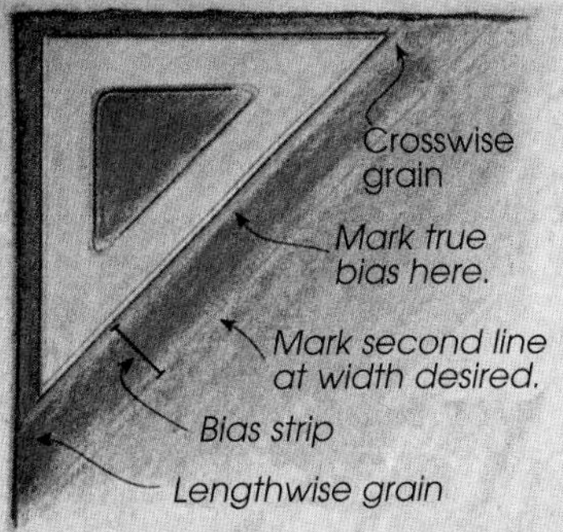

When you're sewing bias bindings, the single most critical step for success is establishing the fabric's true bias. The term *bias* refers to any line or cut that intersects the fabric at an angle to the lengthwise grain, but only the *true bias* angles across the straight grain at an exact 45 degrees. My favorite method for establishing the true bias almost guarantees success and involves measuring and marking with an isosceles right triangle—one with two sides equal in length and a long leg joining them—which is sold in art-supply and stationery stores. You'll also need a straightedge (I prefer a metal or acrylic straightedge to a wooden ruler, which may be warped). And if you use a rotary cutter, you'll need a cutter and mat.

Begin by spreading the fabric, right side up, on the cutting mat. Straighten and smooth the fabric so it lies flat and the crossgrain yarns are perpendicular to the lengthwise yarns (if the fabric's yarns are fine and the grainline difficult to see, use a magnifying glass). Align one short edge of the triangle with the lengthwise grain, which may or may not be a selvage. Align the other short edge with the crossgrain, a little below the top of the fabric, since that edge may not be cut straight. The long edge identifies the true bias. Hold the triangle firmly and chalk-mark the bias along the triangle's long edge.

To make a bias strip, first make two marks at a strip width from the chalked line at each end. Then, using the straightedge, chalk a second line parallel to the first. (If you're marking very long strips, for the sake of accuracy, align the straightedge with the base of the triangle, hold the ruler firmly, and mark the bias along the straightedge.) Repeat to mark additional strips and cut the strips on the marked lines. —C.S.

the more difficult it is to sew and shape smoothly around a curved edge, although a tiny ⅛-in. binding also requires some practice.

Begin with a bias strip four times the finished binding's width plus 1 in. (see "Establishing the true bias" on p. 61 for directions on cutting bias strips). For example, for a finished ¼-in.-wide binding, begin with a 2-in.-wide bias strip. Then prepare the strip for binding and sewing as shown in the top left drawing on the facing page. Following are a few tips for its construction.

Whenever pressing the strip, use a press cloth made from a piece of organza. This fabric is stiff yet transparent so you can see exactly what you're pressing and avoid unwanted creases.

When you've pinned the bias in place, examine the pinned strip to be sure it will wrap smoothly around the neckline edge. You may need to remove it to press and shape it further.

The accuracy of the first thread-marked line (step 5) is critical to the binding's finished appearance because it determines the evenness and width of the completed binding. Rather than relying on my tape measure, I use an old-fashioned cardboard gauge with a ¼-in. notch cut in one end to mark the line with pins before I thread-trace it. The second marked line in step 6 indicates the binding's finished width on the inside of the garment. After marking these lines, trim any excess at the strip's raw edge and ends.

If you don't trim the excess on the neckline's raw edge in step 7, the finished binding will be wider than ¼ in. and a close-fitting neckline will be too tight.

Just before the final stitching (step 10), examine the binding to make sure it's ripple-free, exactly ¼ in. wide, and even in width. Adjust it as needed if it isn't. Then permanently sew the binding, remove the bastings and thread tracings, and lightly press the neckline from the right side with a press cloth and steam. Voilà—you're finished! □

---

*Claire B. Shaeffer, author of* Couture Sewing Techniques, *just published by The Taunton Press, teaches couture techniques at the College of the Desert in Palm Desert, CA.*

*A finished bias binding (above) is elegant on both the wrong (top) and right (bottom) side of the garment. The button loop adds a lovely detail to the opening.*

## Making a button loop

To make a button loop like the one in the photo above, start with a strip cut on the true bias 1 in. wide by about 4 in. long. Fold the strip in half lengthwise with right sides together, and position the strip under the presser foot with the folded edge to the right and ⅛ in. from the needle. Set the stitch length to 20 sts/in. and, holding the threads behind the needle, begin stitching. Once you can grab the strip, stretch it as much as possible with both hands while stitching, which will narrow the tube so you'll be stitching about ¹⁄₁₆ in. from the folded edge. At the end, make the tube a little wider, like a funnel, so you can turn it right side out.

Trim the seam allowance to a scant ⅛ in., thread a tapestry needle with a short, knotted length of buttonhole twist, and anchor the knot at the folded edge of the funnel end. Insert the needle through the tube and pull the tube right side out.

Wet the strip, squeeze it out in a towel, stretch it as much as possible, and pin one end to a pressing board. Make sure the seam is straight. Stretch the strip again as much as possible, pin the other end, and let the strip air dry (don't press it). —C.S.

## Making a staystitching template

*When working with a fabric that distorts easily, placing a template of wax paper under the neckline enables you to preserve the neckline's shape as you staystitch.*

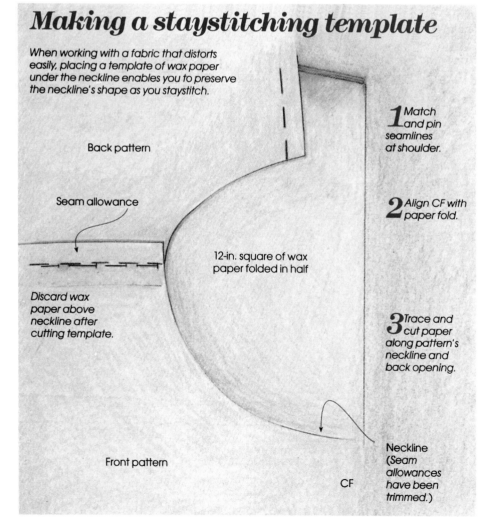

Back pattern

Seam allowance

Discard wax paper above neckline after cutting template.

Front pattern

12-in. square of wax paper folded in half

**1** Match and pin seamlines at shoulder.

**2** Align CF with paper fold.

**3** Trace and cut paper along pattern's neckline and back opening.

Neckline (Seam allowances have been trimmed.)

CF

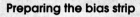

## Preparing the bias strip

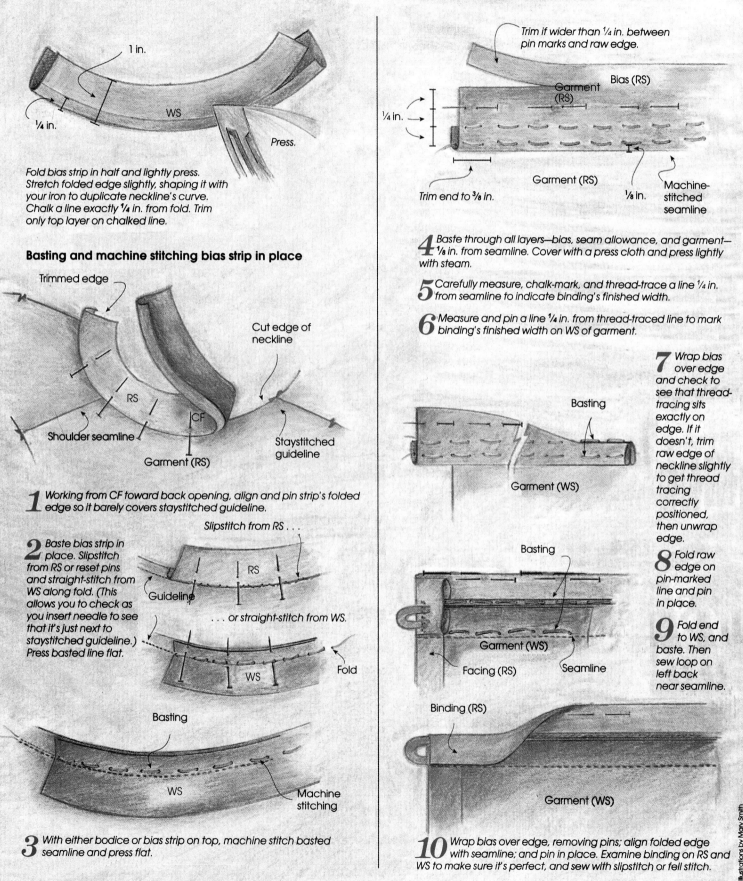

1 in.

¼ in.

WS

Press.

Fold bias strip in half and lightly press. Stretch folded edge slightly, shaping it with your iron to duplicate neckline's curve. Chalk a line exactly ¼ in. from fold. Trim only top layer on chalked line.

## Basting and machine stitching bias strip in place

Trimmed edge

Cut edge of neckline

RS

CF

Shoulder seamline

Garment (RS)

Staystitched guideline

*1* Working from CF toward back opening, align and pin strip's folded edge so it barely covers staystitched guideline.

*2* Baste bias strip in place. Slipstitch from RS or reset pins and straight-stitch from WS along fold. (This allows you to check as you insert needle to see that it's just next to staystitched guideline.) Press basted line flat.

Slipstitch from RS . . .

RS

Guideline

. . . or straight-stitch from WS.

WS

Fold

Basting

WS

Machine stitching

*3* With either bodice or bias strip on top, machine stitch basted seamline and press flat.

## Making the bias for binding

Trim if wider than ¼ in. between pin marks and raw edge.

Bias (RS)

Garment (RS)

¼ in.

Trim end to ⅜ in.

⅛ in.

Machine-stitched seamline

Garment (RS)

*4* Baste through all layers—bias, seam allowance, and garment—⅛ in. from seamline. Cover with a press cloth and press lightly with steam.

*5* Carefully measure, chalk-mark, and thread-trace a line ¼ in. from seamline to indicate binding's finished width.

*6* Measure and pin a line ¼ in. from thread-traced line to mark binding's finished width on WS of garment.

*7* Wrap bias over edge and check to see that thread-tracing sits exactly on edge. If it doesn't, trim raw edge of neckline slightly to get thread tracing correctly positioned, then unwrap edge.

Basting

Garment (WS)

*8* Fold raw edge on pin-marked line and pin in place.

*9* Fold end to WS, and baste. Then sew loop on left back near seamline.

Basting

Garment (WS)

Facing (RS)

Seamline

Binding (RS)

Garment (WS)

*10* Wrap bias over edge, removing pins; align folded edge with seamline; and pin in place. Examine binding on RS and WS to make sure it's perfect, and sew with slipstitch or fell stitch.

Illustrations by Mary Smith

# Shaping a Perfect Sleeve Cap

## Bias strips, machine stitching, and steam shrinking cup fabric for a smooth set

*by Shermane B. Fouché*

*The perfectly shaped sleeve cap results from easing it onto a stretched bias strip of interlining. Voilà—no puckers or gathers!*

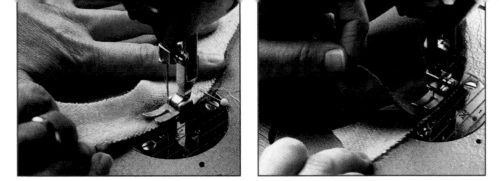

**Stitch bias wool strip to the seamline:** *Center the strip between sleeve notches, with raw edges even. Using a slightly longer than normal stitch length (8 to 10 sts/in.), sew just inside the seamline toward the seam allowance. Start at the top center (marked by a pin) and work toward a notch, pulling the strip as much as it will stretch (left). The strip gathers the cap when it relaxes. Then, flip the sleeve and strip over and stitch the other side of the cap, with the fabric on top (right). The results are like magic: The cap starts easing already.*

**Stitch the seamline and gather with your finger:** *Add more ease by delaying the fabric feed as you stitch again. Press down with your finger behind the foot (above). The fabric gathers in front of the finger. Gather 2 in. at a time, then release.*

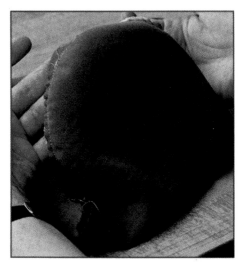

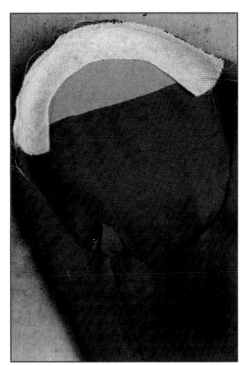

**Shape the wool strip to the cap:** *Work the ease along the seamline, shaping the wool strip into the cap body (above). The cap is already taking great shape. On the inside (right), in addition to the fusible interfacing, the wool adds body to the cap, but neither shows on the right side.*

**Steam the cap:** *Place the cap on the large curved end of a padded wooden sleeve board and steam, as the author shows, above. Press only the seam allowances.*

*h*ave you ever gathered a jacket sleeve cap and ended up with lumps and puckers that wouldn't ease in? With the rounder, less structured shoulder shaping in jackets today, easing the cap just the right amount is more critical than ever. The way I ease a cap takes advantage of the stretch and recovery qualities of a bias fabric strip for a smooth and even finish, avoiding the puckering that results from double lines of gathering stitches. After stretching, machine stitching, and steam shrinking, the bias strip gathers the cap so well that no further easing is needed before setting the sleeve into the jacket (see the photo on the facing page). It works for set-in sleeves on jackets and coats, including those made of smooth, firm fabrics that resist easing, such as wool gabardine.

Today's softer jacket silhouette requires only a slight lift in the sleeve cap, with the total circumference of the sleeve armscye often only 2 in. larger than the garment armscye. The ease extends about 2½ in. down from the shoulder line in front and 3½ in. down from the shoulder line in back. The shape of the sleeve cap also affects its appearance: for a well-shaped jacket shoulder, choose a relatively tall, narrow cap.

In the sequence of photos above, I'm using my easing technique on a wool crepe; test it on various fabrics, both easy and difficult to sew.

To add body to the cap area, first interface the cap of the sleeve from notch to notch with fusible tricot, placing the bias of the tricot on the straight grain of the sleeve. (See the photo directly above). Mark the center top (patterns usually have a dot) with a pin.

Cut a 1½-in.-wide bias strip of Armo woven wool interlining (available from tailoring suppliers such as Oregon Tailor Supply, 2123 S.E. Division St., Portland, OR 97242; 800-678-2457), twice as long as the measurement from notch to notch of the sleeve. Cut in two. The wool is soft, so its edges won't show on the right side, and it shrinks when steamed. For lighter-weight garments such as silk, try using bias strips of lightweight gabardine in place of the Armo wool.

After gathering, the completed sleeve is ready to be inserted into the jacket. The result, as shown on the facing page: a perfectly shaped sleeve. □

*Shermane Fouché is a professional dressmaker in San Francisco, CA. The patterns for the clothing shown here are available from her at PO Box 410273, San Francisco, CA 94141.*

Clothing manufacturers often make buttonholes in silk on non-industrial machines. Their secret: Spread the zigzag stitches to keep the buttonhole pliable, and use fine thread, needle, and interfacing. The buttonhole foot shown has a center prong for holding cording in place.

# *Buttonholes for Silk*

## Fine thread and soft interfacing complement a fluid fabric

*by Claire B. Shaeffer*

From *Threads* magazine (April 1993) 46:38-41

Soft, lustrous silks are so inviting. It's easy to imagine a blouse made from a shimmery, satiny charmeuse, a bright colorful crepe de chine, or a beautifully textured jacquard. However, the thought of the final construction step—making the buttonholes—often gives us cold feet. And little wonder. The soft silk layers slide across each other under the needle, little dimples grin at each end of the buttonholes, and somehow the satin stitching just doesn't look right.

Clothing manufacturers of high-priced ready-to-wear face the same problems. While there are industrial machines that only make buttonholes, they're so expensive that many American manufacturers have their seamstresses make the buttonholes on regular home sewing machines. Their standard for excellence may surprise you: The zigzag stitches are spread apart (photo on the facing page), rather than lying tightly side by side as in satin stitching. This construction complements the drape of the fabric and makes the buttonholes unobtrusive. Here's how to fine-tune your technique to achieve the same quality on silks, as well as silky synthetics and lightweight microfibers.

The success of your buttonholes depends on many elements, but two—interfacing and thread—are particularly important. The interfacing directly affects the quality of the work while the thread affects the aesthetics.

### It's better to sample first

I've made lots of silk blouses with hundreds of buttonholes, but I didn't realize until a couple of years ago that I had been putting the cart before the horse. I'd assemble the garment up to the buttonholes, then I'd make the buttonhole samples. If I found it impossible to make good-looking buttonholes, I wasn't left with many alternatives.

I strongly suggest that you make samples *before* you cut out the garment, while you still have the option to change the design, use a different interfacing, or do away with the buttonholes altogether. If you find that attractive buttonholes are impossible, you can select another type of closure. For example, you could consider making a small keyhole opening in the blouse back and use loops instead of buttonholes. You can also hide the buttons and buttonholes under a placket, as many patterns do today.

### Interfacing for stability

A buttonhole in slippery fabric needs interfacing to add body to the fabric, to prevent the finished buttonhole from gap-ping or stretching, and to stabilize the buttonhole area for stitching. If the buttonhole isn't stabilized, the fabric "tunnels," forming cupped areas under each line of zigzags (or bead), and the beads narrow. The fabric can also shift so the space between the beads is uneven and a pucker or pleat forms at the tack at each end of the buttonhole.

The challenge in interfacing silk is to avoid changing the character of the fabric, particularly in the front of the garment where the buttonholes can be seen by all. The interfacing can be slightly crisper or softer than the fabric, but it should not be heavier.

No single interfacing is the best choice for every application, but I like wovens for silk because they are stable both lengthwise and crosswise and don't need further stabilization to prevent gapping of the buttonhole. If you use a knit, you may need to cord the buttonholes (instructions on p. 69).

I preshrink all my interfacings before sewing. Whether it's a fusible or not, I fill a basin with hot tap water, immerse the interfacing gently in the water without agitation, let the water cool, and then hang the interfacing to drip dry or lay it on a towel to dry.

**Fusibles**—There are two low-temperature woven fusibles that work well. Silk can be marred by the high temperatures required by normal fusibles, but I've found that HTC's low-temp. Touch o' Gold (100 percent rayon) works well. If you use a press cloth, you can use a high-temp. fusible; silkweight works well. Both of these interfacings are appropriate for crepe de chine. (For more on the new low-temp. interfacings, see the article on pp. 34-35.)

If you prefer nonwoven fusibles, Dritz's lightweight Shape-Up, HTC's SofTouch, and Pellon's nonwoven for sheers (906F) are good choices, but they all give in the crosswise direction and may need to be stabilized at the buttonhole opening.

Stacy's Easy Knit, Dritz's Knit Fuze, and HTC's Whisper Weft are slightly heavier and work better on the heavier silks, such as jacquards and charmeuse, than on crepe de chine. With the exception of Whisper Weft, they have crosswise stretch.

**Nonfusibles**—When you can't or don't want to use a fusible, try these suggestions: silk or polyester organza, self-fabric, HTC's Sewin' Sheer, and fashion fabrics—such as silk broadcloth or polyester chiffon—all work well. Self-fabric would match your fabric exactly in drape and color. You'll need to baste these interfacings in place with long hand stitches so they won't shift during sewing.

**Where to apply the interfacing**—Where you apply the interfacing depends on the effect you want. I usually interface the front facings so the silk remains smooth on the right side, and interface both layers of cuffs for crispness. The best way to check how an interfacing works and where to place it is to make lots of samples, especially with the fusibles. I know this is a dull task, but it's a cheap and easy way to gain lots of experience quickly. Besides, you can save the samples for when you're sewing future designs on similar fabrics.

Experiment with swatches of your fabric by applying interfacing that's been cut on the lengthwise or crosswise grain and even on the bias. The interfacing may look fine when applied to the garment, as patterns often suggest, or may work better if applied to the facing, particularly if the interfacing stiffens the fabric.

### Selecting thread

Buttonholes on lightweight silks need fine thread that won't overwhelm them. My favorite threads (in no special order) are Mettler's 60/2 fine embroidery cotton (see *Basics, Threads* No. 46, p. 16) for an explanation of thread weights); silk sewing thread size A or 50/3; Coats & Clark's extra-fine Dual Duty (cotton-covered polyester); and DMC's all-cotton 50/2 embroidery thread. (DMC thread comes in almost 200 colors that match DMC's embroidery floss. The floss is common in needlework shops. You can match your fabric to a floss color, then order the 50/2 by mail if the retailer doesn't carry the thread. See "Sources for thread and interfacing" on p. 69.)

The threads vary in luster; silk thread has the most shine while the Dual Duty has the least. If you can't find a color that seems to match your fabric exactly, it's well worth trying some samples in close shades. Colors can look different when stitched on buttonholes, and you may be surprised by the one you like best. ⇨

*The challenge when interfacing silk is to avoid changing the fabric's drapey character.*

## Needles

You'll also need to use a fine needle (to match the thread). The brand of needle that you select depends on the type of sewing machine you have and what its manufacturer recommends. Sewing machines are precise instruments, and using the wrong needle can damage the sewing mechanism. You should consult your local sewing machine dealer before you change needle brands.

When sewing on machines that use Schmetz needles, the needle you're most likely to have on hand is a universal needle (H point). I suggest starting with a size 70/10, which is finer than the 80/12 recommended for most fabrics. If the universal needle produces puckers in your fabric, try a sharper point in the same size, a denim needle with an HJ point. If you're trying to sew on a silky microfiber, and the sharp point doesn't work, the ball-point stretch needle (HS point) might do the trick.

If you're sewing on a machine that uses Singer needles, I suggest trying a Red (sharp) or Yellow (ball-point) Band needle in size 65/9 or 75/11. Singer does not offer a denim needle in a fine size.

## Stabilizing for sewing

Sewing samples not only tells you whether you've matched the fabric to the interfacing, thread, and needle; it indicates whether you need to further stabilize the layers for sewing. Silk is still going to slide while you're making the buttonhole. Here are a few techniques you can try to keep the fabric taut:

*Holding the fabric taut* on each side of the buttonhole foot with your fingers when stitching sometimes works.

*Hand basting an oval around each buttonhole location* has worked the best for me. Baste through all layers about ¼ in. from the marked buttonhole line. If the fabric creeps a lot, baste the oval twice so the stitches of the second basting fill the spaces of the first basting (see the photo below).

*Baste a layer of Sulky's water-soluble stabilizer to the facing side of the garment.* This stabilizer looks like clear plastic and it dissolves when wet. To remove the stabilizer after stitching the buttonhole, steam the stabilizer, then pull it away gently while it is still warm. This works, but the stabilizer that remains in the zigzag stitches does make the buttonhole stiffer.

You should also be aware that glue-basting the layers together or fusing a web between the layers is likely to add undesirable stiffness.

## Troubleshooting samples

Making a buttonhole is a two-step process, so I recommend making samples in two steps. First adjust the stitch length until you get a line of forward zigzag stitching that is spaced just right. (Most machines with automatic buttonholes don't allow you to adjust the stitch width, but you can check the spacing by adjusting the stitch length.) Then work the right side of the buttonhole, again adjusting the stitch length until the stitches match those in the first bead.

Buttonholes need a tighter bobbin tension than regular stitching to pull the knots slightly to the underside of the fabric. On some sewing machines, you can pass the thread through an eye on the finger of the bobbin case to increase the tension. You can also increase tension by tightening the screw on the bobbin case slightly. (Consult your machine manual for further instructions.)

Set the machine for stitching the left bead, then set the stitch length. I begin with a stitch length of about .5mm, not 0, which would make satin stitches. The satin stitch makes a stiffer, heavier buttonhole, which can easily overwhelm a drapey silk (see the photo on the facing page). Stitch several inches and examine the bead. Are there skipped stitches? Does the tension or stitch length need to be adjusted? Does the fabric tunnel, making the bead narrower?

Skipped stitches often indicate a need for a different size or type of needle. It may be that static is building up on the needle, especially if you are working with a synthetic fabric. The skipping may go away if you apply a needle lubricant to the thread on the spool and between the tension discs.

If the fabric tunnels, that means it isn't crisp enough, so place a piece of water-soluble stabilizer between the fabric and feed dog(s).

If the stitch length looks a little long, but the buttonhole lies flat and unpuck-

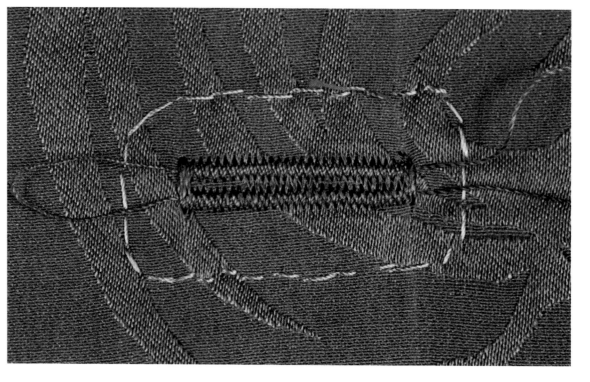

*Two lines of **hand basting** hold fabric layers together so they won't slip and slide during stitching. (The second pass fills the spaces between the stitches of the first.) **Matching sewing thread serves as cording:** The thread fills the spaces between the zigzags. Pull the cording ends to tighten the loop, then knot on the wrong side to prevent the slashed edges of the buttonhole from stretching and gapping.*

*The stitch length is critical.* Zigzag stitches packed tightly side by side (stitch length nearly 0, top) totally stiffen the fabric. Stitches that are too far apart (center) leave the edges open to raveling. Stitches spread just right (bottom) cover the fabric well and prevent fraying.

ered, you can cord the buttonhole with two strands of matching thread (as described in "Cording a buttonhole" at right) to make the stitching look less sparse, rather than trying a shorter stitch length.

Because the feed dogs move backward to make the second bead, the stitches are made differently, and they may look different. You can reset the stitch length so the second bead looks the same as the first, but this isn't critical if the buttonhole generally lies flat.

If there is a pleat at either end of the buttonhole, it is a sign that the fabric has shifted. This tells you that the buttonhole needs to be stabilized.

If the buttonhole looks pretty good, stand back about 5 ft. and evaluate the results. The buttonhole should harmonize with the design, not stand out like a sore thumb. Now you're ready to cut out the garment, assured that good buttonholes are possible. And here's something to keep in mind for further reassurance: The buttonholes don't all need to be perfect. The ones in the upper part of the blouse or dress will be scrutinized more closely than the ones near the bottom.

Viewers will never see the buttonholes that are tucked into a skirt. □

*Claire B. Shaeffer teaches classes on clothing construction at the College of the Desert in Palm Desert, CA, and nationally. She is working on a book of couture techniques for The Taunton Press.*

### Sources for thread and interfacing

**Professional Sewing Supplies**
PO Box 14272
Seattle, WA 98114-4272
(206) 324-8823
*Silkweight interfacing (4 colors). For catalog, send SASE. Samples, $1.*

**Things Japanese**
9805 N.E. 116th St., Suite 7160
Kirkland, WA 98034
(206) 821-2287
*50/3 silk thread in 171 colors. Sample card, $12; catalog, $2.*

**TreadleArt**
25834 Narbonne Ave.
Lomita, CA 90717
(310) 534-5122
*DMC 50/2 and Metrosene 60/2 thread, and Solvy water-soluble stabilizer. Will match color swatches. Catalog, $3.*

## Cording a buttonhole

Cording a buttonhole with thread is like staying an edge with tape: the thread keeps the buttonhole edges from stretching. When you can't use heavier interfacing because it would change the drape around the buttonhole, cording with thread is a good solution.

The buttonhole foot of most machines has a prong or hook in the front just for cording. You loop the thread over the prong and run the ends under the foot in the grooves meant for the lines of zigzags. Silk buttonholes generally need only a single strand of thread or cord, but you can double the thread if you just want to fill the spaces between stitches.

Cut the thread so that when it's looped, it is longer than the buttonhole and easy to thread into a needle. Drape the thread over the prong and under the foot, then hold the ends gently so the tension keeps the thread centered in the zigzag stitching and taut over the prong. The foot pulls the thread loop forward as it goes down the left side of the buttonhole (going forward). Keep the tension just tight enough to keep the thread straight on the right side of the buttonhole. The forward end will have a loose loop (photo on the facing page).

When the buttonhole is finished, pull the ends so the loop flattens against the bar tack. If you're cording the buttonhole just to fill the spaces between zigzag stitches, you don't have to anchor and knot the ends. Just carefully pull the thread taut and cut close to the stitching; the ends will disappear into the stitching.

If you're cording the buttonhole for stability and the thread ends are short, thread the ends into a regular or self-threading (calyx-eyed) needle (available in the notions area of fabric stores). Insert the needle into the fabric at one end of the bar tack and run it to the wrong side of the garment. Knot the ends together firmly next to the fabric with a tailors' knot (see *Basics, Threads* No. 46, p. 16). Because you're counting on the thread to maintain the size of the opening, the thread shouldn't have any slack. Trim the ends and you're finished. — C.B.S.

**Photo by Yvonne Taylor**

# *Fine Points for Perfect Pockets*

## Careful marking and the right interfacing make problem welts foolproof

*by Linda Wakefield*

*Both traditional double-welt pockets and the single-welt variations shown here are easy to make well when you know how. The author is an old hand at them, and she shares her secrets herein.*

*d*o you cringe at the thought of making a welt pocket? Many sewers do, but I can hardly let a garment go by without figuring out some way to work a pocket into it, and I usually include several. The difference could be my method for making them, which virtually guarantees success. On the following pages, I'll describe in detail how I make regular inset double-welt pockets, as well as a variation which looks like a single welt. It's also completely inset into the garment fabric, unlike the traditional single welt, which sits on top of the garment layer, covering the opening. You can see it in the photo on the facing page. Because they are fully inset, the finished pockets have no visible stitches and don't need top or edge stitching if they are pressed well. You can add stitching for decoration, of course, but it's nice not to have to.

Whether or not you've designed the garment that you're making, you ought to give the pockets careful consideration before you plunge right in, to be sure that the ones you make will turn out looking good and will be comfortable to use. So let's start at the beginning, with planning and design.

## Planning pockets

The functional aspect of a pocket is only part of the story, and it's not necessarily even the main part. Pockets are also an opportunity to exhibit fine workmanship and add interesting detail. They can be prim, subtle, playful, decorative, even flamboyant. You can design pockets to complement a garment, or you can design a garment around a pocket. I usually prefer pockets that are both functional and decorative.

**Position and size**—The first point that I consider for all of my pockets is the placement and size of the opening. For exterior welt pockets that will fit the entire hand, I usually prefer to make a vertical pocket opening (as opposed to horizontal or diagonal) because it hangs shut and doesn't gap even with frequent use. I use horizontal openings for interior pockets, for shallow "fingertip" pockets (so the contents don't spill out), and simply for variety's sake.

One natural resting position for the hands is approximately at the hip bone, 2 to 3 in. below the waist and about halfway between center front and the side seam. The opening of a woman's pocket should be about 5½ to 6 in., or about 1 in. greater than the width of the hand, to allow for the thickness of the hand.

**Design**—The standard in traditional tailoring is for the pocket parts to match the garment at every stripe or plaid as if the pocket wasn't there to interfere with the flow of the garment fabric. My method works perfectly well for this approach, but I always think of pockets as decorative elements, so I cut almost all my welt strips on the bias. Most fabric folds better on the bias than on the straight or cross-grain, but primarily I prefer the way the bias looks. As you'll see below, I interface the strips to stabilize them, so they'll act like grain-straight fabric no matter how they're cut, but I enjoy playing with the texture and pattern variations that bias strips can create against an on-grain garment. Plaids and stripes form chevrons when they meet on the diagonal, and even linen and tussah textures look better to me when they aren't parallel to the background fabric. The wrong side of the fabric can also provide an interesting interplay of texture or shade, the subtle differences providing contrast and harmony at the same time.

Another traditional standard is for the pocket lining to match the garment, so there's no contrast when the pocket opens. But tailored doesn't have to mean boring! I like to use contrasting linings that peak out invitingly between the welts, as long as they also fill the other lining requirements, described below.

## Interfacing

Interfacing is essential for supporting the pocket area on the garment, and for keeping the welts looking crisp. But don't confuse interfacing with stiffening; the two are not necessarily the same. The correct interfacing for your fabric will have just enough weight and crispness to support your pocket, and will visibly improve your results without changing the flow, drape, or softness of your fabric. I use all kinds of interfacing, both fusible and sew-in, except nonwovens, which I don't trust (they remind me of tissue—I'd rather use a knit or woven that will act like fabric). I encourage you to test your choices before committing yourself. Here are my favorites:

Weft-insertion fusibles, like Whisper Weft, Armo Weft, and Suit Maker, are good basic interfacings. They provide perfect support without over-interfacing, and they're completely stable in at least one direction—perfect for stabilizing bias welt strips. They're good for suit weights and heavier fabrics such as wool flannels

and coating wools, and are available in white, natural, light gray, charcoal, and sometimes black. Your color choice should respect the opacity of the garment fabric. For instance, natural could be the least visible under white fabric. It's the same principle as wearing "nude" undergarments under white clothing.

Fusible knit interfacings, like Easy Knit and Knit Fuse, among others, provide good, delicate support for lightweight fabrics where the relative bulk of most weft insertions is not desirable. I've used these on voiles, gauze, and even China silk without spoiling the drape; they're not just for knits. But because they have some stretch in every direction, I don't use knits to interface welt strips, even if I've used one to support the pocket opening.

Woven, nonfusible interfacings can

work well, for either the welts or the pocket area, when basted into place. Tailors' canvas, such as Armo Rite, provides great body and support. Its loose weave keeps garments flexible without adding stiffness. I've used this as the garment interfacing for bulky bomber-type jackets, under handwovens and leathers, and as the underlining for pieced cotton jackets.

Less bulky woven nonfusibles, like Veriform and other brands, can provide soft to crisp support for lighter fabrics. For sheers, lace, and open weaves, organdy or organza work beautifully as interfacing and underlining.

## Linings

Pocket linings need to be lightweight but strong, so they neither add bulk nor wear out. Check to make sure your choice doesn't show through the garment fabric. I've used China silk, sheath lining, and broadcloth. For a basic pocket into which you can put your whole hand, I use two pieces 8 by 10 in.

If the garment is long enough, the pocket lining should allow the hand to slant downward. But if the garment is short, like a waist-length baseball or bomber jacket, the lining will be horizontal, more of a tunnel than a bag. In any case, I cut simple rectangles for all my pocket linings, then I round off the corners as I stitch the lining into a pocket, so they don't collect dust. I trim around the stitches, then overcast the edges. ⇨

When you cut out the lining fabric, you can make it in one piece or two. You can cut one large piece that folds in half (either at the pocket bottom or side) to form both layers of the pocket. Or you can cut two identically shaped pieces and stitch them on all sides. In this case, the two layers needn't be the same fabric; the layer that will be visible through the opening can be selected for color or pattern without requiring a piece large enough for the whole pocket. The other layer should be selected for thinness and durability. You could also piece or appliqué a decorative fabric to a fold-over lining so it falls right behind the opening when complete, as long as the combination isn't too bulky.

## Construction

The construction steps I use for welt pockets are shown in the drawings below. The single-welt variation is the same process except for the size and initial positioning of the welts; these are shown on p. 50. Here are some fine points to consider as you read the instructions.

**Dimensions**—With either style, the opening dimensions are up to you. For the double-welt pocket, I've given dimensions for a 1- by 6-in. finished pocket, which is what I typically use for an outside, full-hand pocket. If you want to make a different size, simply allow 1 in. extra length for the welts, beyond their finished size, and cut each strip exactly four times the finished width you want for each welt. So, for ⅜-in. welts (which would make a ¾-in.-wide pocket), you'd cut two 1½-in.-wide welt strips, each 1 in.

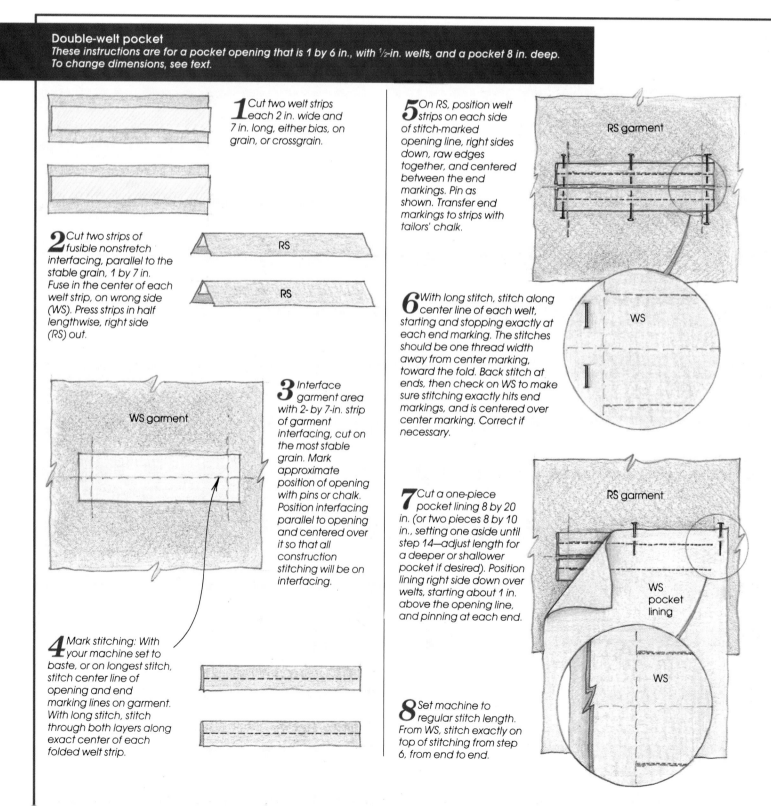

**Double-welt pocket**

*These instructions are for a pocket opening that is 1 by 6 in., with ½-in. welts, and a pocket 8 in. deep. To change dimensions, see text.*

**1** Cut two welt strips each 2 in. wide and 7 in. long, either bias, on grain, or crossgrain.

**2** Cut two strips of fusible nonstretch interfacing, parallel to the stable grain, 1 by 7 in. Fuse in the center of each welt strip, on wrong side (WS). Press strips in half lengthwise, right side (RS) out.

**3** Interface garment area with 2- by 7-in. strip of garment interfacing, cut on the most stable grain. Mark approximate position of opening with pins or chalk. Position interfacing parallel to opening and centered over it so that all construction stitching will be on interfacing.

**4** Mark stitching: With your machine set to baste, or on longest stitch, stitch center line of opening and end marking lines on garment. With long stitch, stitch through both layers along exact center of each folded welt strip.

**5** On RS, position welt strips on each side of stitch-marked opening line, right sides down, raw edges together, and centered between the end markings. Pin as shown. Transfer end markings to strips with tailors' chalk.

**6** With long stitch, stitch along center line of each welt, starting and stopping exactly at each end marking. The stitches should be one thread width away from center marking, toward the fold. Back stitch at ends, then check on WS to make sure stitching exactly hits end markings, and is centered over center marking. Correct if necessary.

**7** Cut a one-piece pocket lining 8 by 20 in. (or two pieces 8 by 10 in., setting one aside until step 14—adjust length for a deeper or shallower pocket if desired). Position lining right side down over welts, starting about 1 in. above the opening line, and pinning at each end.

**8** Set machine to regular stitch length. From WS, stitch exactly on top of stitching from step 6, from end to end.

longer than the length of your pocket. The practical lower limit for welt width with this technique is ¼ in. each, or possibly ³⁄₁₆ in., if you're careful. For the single-welt variation, just double the width of the visible welt, and add 1 in. for seam allowances. The length is determined the same way as for double welts.

**Mark stitching**—One of the things you'll notice right away in these instructions is how various steps start with making lines of machine stitches, which serve either as position markers, or as guides for subsequent stitches. This is the most accurate way to mark both side of the fabric, so please try it. My machine has a ½-in. basting stitch, which I use for marking the pocket position on the garment. For the other marking stitches, I set my machine at its longest regular stitch, six stitches per inch, or about 4mm. Use this setting in place of machine basting, if your machine doesn't have that feature.

The way my method ensures that your welts will meet in the middle of the pocket opening is by using the welt's seam allowances as layout guides when you stitch them to the garment. This works only if you carefully cut the welt strips to *exactly* four times the welt's finished width, and then mark-stitch down the exact center of the folded, interfaced strip. (See step 4 in the drawing on the facing page.) This line of stitching is the guide for attaching the welt to the garment.

To make sure the mark stitching just described isn't seen when the welt is

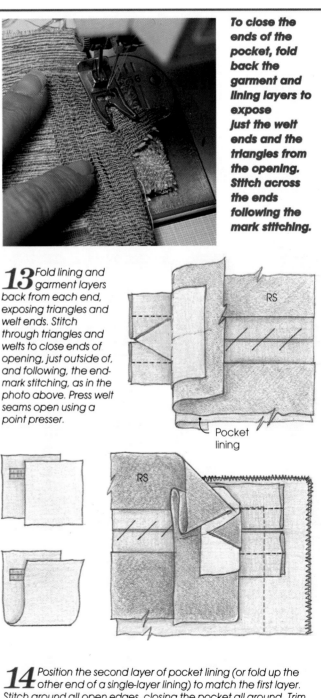

Clip to the ends of the stitching lines, cutting the garment and lining layers separately, without cutting the welts. Fold back the triangles as shown.

To close the ends of the pocket, fold back the garment and lining layers to expose just the welt ends and the triangles from the opening. Stitch across the ends following the mark stitching.

**9** Slash through all layers along center marking, starting and stopping 1 in. from each end of stitching line. Cutting through only the lining on RS, and only the garment on WS (don't cut welts), snip from slash ends to each end of stitching from step 8, forming triangles, as in photo above.

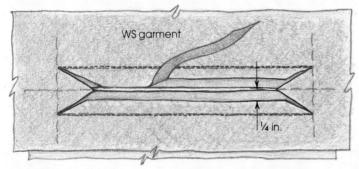

WS garment

¼ in.

**10** Trim away seam allowance on garment layer to grade seam, leaving ¼-in. allowance.

**11** Turn lining to WS through opening, tucking welt ends through openings at each end, between lining and garment triangles— don't handle triangles more than necessary. Arrange welts in center of opening, triangles pointing outward away from opening. Finger-press open garment and lining seams along welts.

RS garment

**12** From RS, hand baste the welt edges together on center of opening. Don't remove basting until garment is complete.

**13** Fold lining and garment layers back from each end, exposing triangles and welt ends. Stitch through triangles and welts to close ends of opening, just outside of, and following, the end-mark stitching, as in the photo above. Press welt seams open using a point presser.

RS

Pocket lining

RS

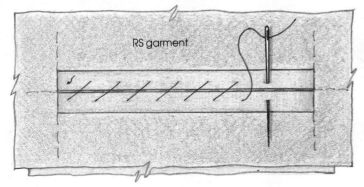

**14** Position the second layer of pocket lining (or fold up the other end of a single-layer lining) to match the first layer. Stitch around all open edges, closing the pocket all around. Trim and overcast edges. It's usually not necessary to catch welt seam allowances or triangles in pocket stitching, but if pocket sags, stitch the top to the upper welt seam, close to the opening seamline. Remove mark stitching.

turned to its finished position, the construction stitching needs to conceal it. To do that, the instructions (step 6, p. 72) say to stitch the welt down one thread's width toward the fold side of the center line. This works perfectly for me, but some people have found that this creates a small gap between the welt folds after turning, because the construction stitching isn't on the center lines anymore. If this is the case on your initial sample (you *are* making a sample, aren't you?), simply make the initial center-line stitch-

ing on your next pocket one thread's width off center towards the seam allowance. That way the next line will be exactly on center.

**Sewing straight lines**—One secret to the success of this method is being able to sew perfectly straight lines, both as thread markings and in construction, particularly when you're stitching one line on top of, or right next to, a previous one. Wobbly stitching lines *will* show up in the pocket's final appearance, espe-

cially if you're using a firm, smooth, unforgiving fabric such as gabardine, twill, or broadcloth. One useful technique is to fold in half a piece of notebook paper and use the folded edge as a guide. Slip the fold under the presser foot right up next to the needle, hold it in front and in back on top of the line you want to stitch, and keep the needle hitting the edge as you sew. If you stitch the longer lines in the construction of your pocket this way, you'll be very pleased with the results.

The paper guide can be awkward when you're initially stitching the center of a welt strip. Try marking the line first with chalk or pen, then positioning your fingers firmly on either side of the strip to act as guides as it passes under the foot, so that it feeds in without wobbling.

**Basting welts and cutting corners**—Please take the time to hand baste the welt folds together before you press the opening and stitch down the ends. It only takes a minute or two and, if done with care, will ensure that the welts stay parallel, square, and don't overlap or gap when you're done. Knot the basting thread, and stitch from the right side. Don't remove it until the garment's finished. For the least distortion of the pocket parts, don't press anything until after the triangles are sewn down in step 13, p. 73. I only finger-press the welt strips open before basting. After the triangles are secure, you can press open the long welt seams over a hard, narrow surface, like a point presser, to make sure the seams lie flat.

It's always important to cut right to the corners—not less, and not beyond—when you're turning a stitched box, as in step 9. If you cut too short, the turn won't lie flat, and if you cut into the stitches, the cut will show up on the front. The best way to do this is to position the point of the scissors at the stitches before you close the scissors, rather than snipping towards them. But if you're still nervous about cutting too far, slip a pin diagonally right across the corner stitch so you can't cut through it, even by mistake.

You'll notice (step 9) that I like to cut the center slash in the pocket opening only to within an inch of the ends, so the resulting triangles are long and easy to handle. I think you'll like it, too, but try not to handle the triangles any more than you have to, or they'll fray. Poke the welt ends through the gaps at the ends with the point of your scissors, if necessary. Good luck! □

*Linda Wakefield designs and makes one-of-a-kind garments, and teaches sewing classes in Southern California.*

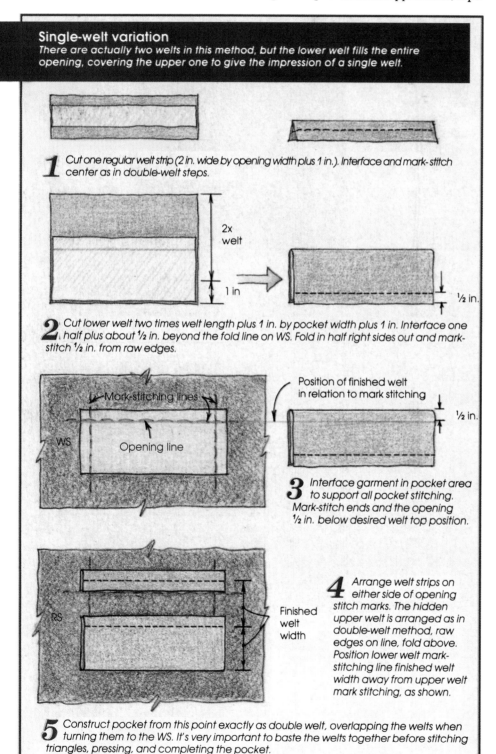

## Single-welt variation
*There are actually two welts in this method, but the lower welt fills the entire opening, covering the upper one to give the impression of a single welt.*

**1** Cut one regular welt strip (2 in. wide by opening width plus 1 in.). Interface and mark-stitch center as in double-welt steps.

2x welt

1 in

½ in.

**2** Cut lower welt two times welt length plus 1 in. by pocket width plus 1 in. Interface one half plus about ½ in. beyond the fold line on WS. Fold in half right sides out and mark-stitch ½ in. from raw edges.

Mark-stitching lines

WS

Opening line

Position of finished welt in relation to mark stitching

½ in.

**3** Interface garment in pocket area to support all pocket stitching. Mark-stitch ends and the opening ½ in. below desired welt top position.

RS

Finished welt width

**4** Arrange welt strips on either side of opening stitch marks. The hidden upper welt is arranged as in double-welt method, raw edges on line, fold above. Position lower welt mark-stitching line finished welt width away from upper welt mark stitching, as shown.

**5** Construct pocket from this point exactly as double welt, overlapping the welts when turning them to the WS. It's very important to baste the welts together before stitching triangles, pressing, and completing the pocket.

# Foolproof Zipper Insertion

## Three steps and a stitching guide guarantee a professional look

*by Elissa Meyrich*

*a*s a sewer who has also worked in the garment industry for years, I'm always fascinated to see how samplemakers approach a sewing task, especially if it's one I've struggled with. Samplemakers make the first wearable versions of a designer's ideas, like the Tamotsu suit at right, for the press, and for shows. Unlike assembly-line factory sewers, samplemakers almost always work from start to finish on a single garment, so, like home sewers, they need to know how to get quick, great-looking results at every construction step. Whether it's a challenging job like setting in a jacket sleeve, or something as basic as inserting a zipper, they al-most always know of a streamlined, "why-didn't-I-think-of-that?" technique.

The mock fly zipper is a good example of how samplemakers pare even basic processes down to their essentials, yet are willing to go to extra lengths to ensure perfect results. In the photo sequence on **pp. 76-77**, you'll see zipper insertion reduced to three quick steps, with a minimum of marking, and minimal reliance on practice and skill. But when it comes to the topstitching, you'll see a device used by many samplemakers: an adhesive stitching guide, made from ordinary office-supply sticky-paper labels, cut to shape and used over and over until the adhesive fails. It makes that last, nerve-wracking step a breeze. ⇨

*A great-looking mock-fly zipper can be easy to make. The samplemaker at Tamotsu who made this suit used the technique described on the following pages, and so can you.*

### The samplemakers' mock fly

It's "mock" because it doesn't have a fly shield—a fabric extension under the zipper— as do men's flys.

You don't have to change the typical sewing pattern's zipper set-up (see drawing below), but these three steps should simplify the instruction sheet, while ensuring that your zipper doesn't peek out of the opening when it's zipped up.

#### Preparing for a mock fly

Make sure the extensions are wide enough to catch in the topstitching you've planned.

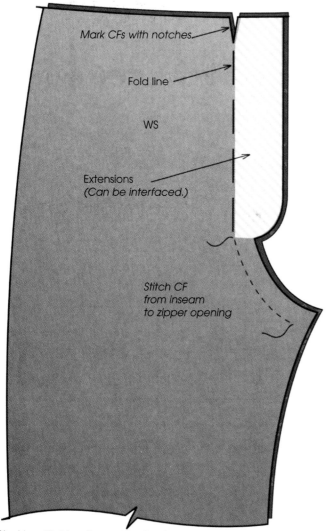

Mark CFs with notches

Fold line

WS

Extensions
(Can be interfaced.)

Stitch CF
from inseam
to zipper opening

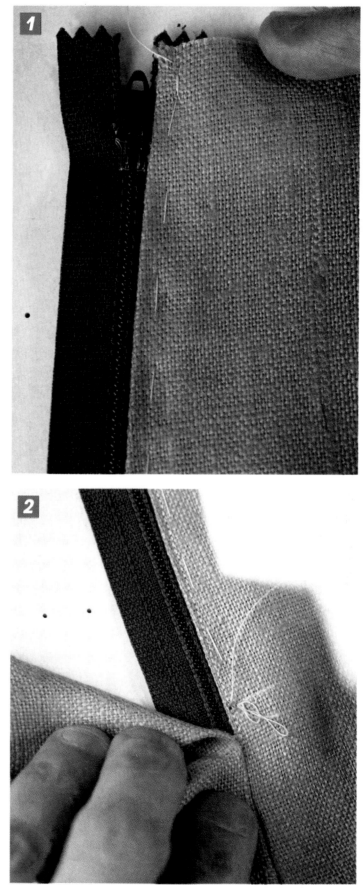

Start by stitching the center-front crotch seam and marking the center front as shown above. Press the underlap fly extension to the wrong side from waist to seam, with the fold line shifted about $1/16$ in. to the extension side of the center-front notch (this helps position the zipper out of sight when you're done).

**1.** Position the closed zipper teeth against the fold, with the bottom stop below the end of the crotch seam and the top stops flush with the waist seamline; baste. (Most samplemakers would skip basting, but it's wisest not to, especially if the fabric is slippery or stretchy.)

**2.** With zipper foot and matching thread (I used contrasting thread for illustration only), stitch close to fold, stopping at crotch seam.

## Step 2: The overlap

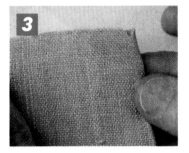

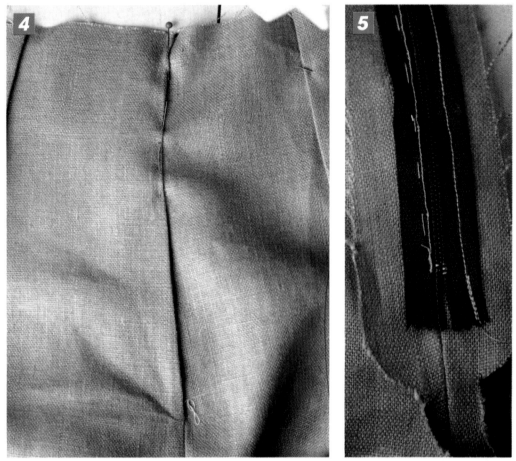

**3.** With your fingers, shift the overlap center-front fold line towards the extension about ⅛ in. at the waist, tapering to nothing at the crotch seam, and press. (This is final insurance against zipper peek-out.)

**4.** Pin the fold over the underlap from top to bottom, matching center-front notches at the waist.

**5.** Turn to the wrong side and pin, then stitch the other side of the zipper tape (with the zipper closed) to the overlap extension only (right-hand stitching line, photo 5). Keep this stitching in the middle of the tape as shown, not next to the teeth. (Finish the extension edges now by overcasting or serging if you haven't done that already.)

## Step 3: Topstitching

**6.** On the right side, and with the zipper still closed, unpin the overlap and stick an adhesive stitching guide along the center front on the overlap side. The guide shown is made from two 4- by 6-in. white office labels stuck together lengthwise and trimmed to the exact finished shape of the topstitching (⅞ in. wide, ending in a smooth curve—copy your favorite pants). Save the peel-away backing for the guide so you can reuse it. The bottom of the curve should fall just below the zipper opening, and below the zipper stop. (Make sure you're not going to hit the stop.) Stitch around the guide using your zipper foot, so you can see the guide clearly.

**7.** Pull off the guide and you're done!

---

*Elissa Meyrich is a garment industry consultant. She teaches at the Parsons School of Design as well as in her store, Sew Fast/Sew Easy.*

# Replacing a Zipper

## An easy alteration can save your pants or skirt

*by Mary A. Roehr*

**2** Removing the zipper: Rip out (remove) the old zipper carefully, marking the sewing lines with chalk, basting thread, or a disappearing marking pen. Also rip and mark the topstitching line of the fly to release the fly facing. Open the parts of the waistband that enclose the upper ends of the zipper.

**1** Familiarizing yourself with the parts of a zipper is the first step towards a successful zipper replacement.

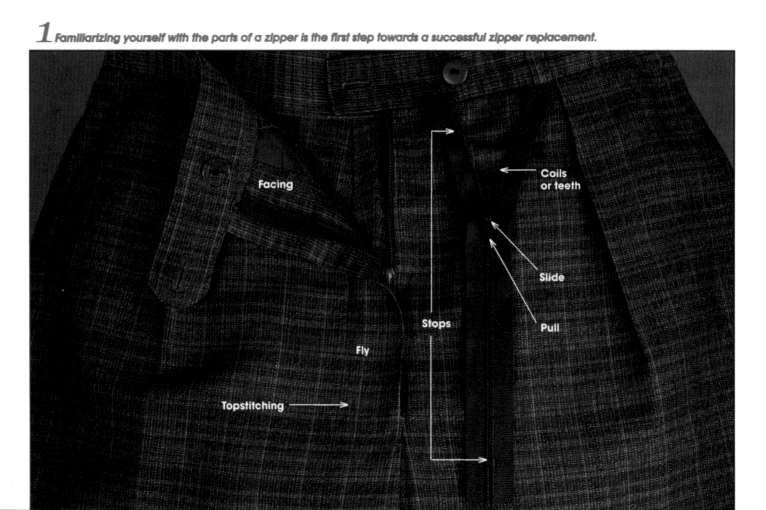

Facing

Coils or teeth

Slide

Pull

Stops

Fly

Topstitching

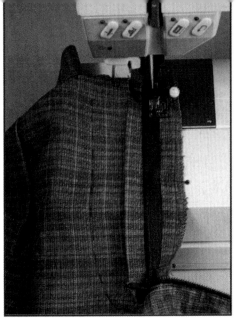

**3** *Replacing the easy side: Positioning the lower zipper stop at bottom of pants opening, pin right side of new zipper in place, with fabric fold close to teeth. Using a zipper foot, stitch from the top down close to the fold, interrupting stitching to move the slide. If stops have been removed from the top of the zipper, take care not to let the slide slip off.*

**4** *Replacing the fly side: Close the zipper and pin or baste over basting line on fly facing (don't catch the outer fabric). The zipper will be face down. Open the zipper and stitch it in place from the top down.*

**5** *Topstitching: From the right side, resew the fly topstitching from the bottom up, following the basting or old stitching line. Add a bar tack below the lower zipper stop, if you desire, with a short , narrow zigzag.*

---

t**he zipper breaks in your favorite pair of pants, but the rest of the garment is perfectly fine. What do you do? When I worked as a custom tailor, my clients paid me up to $15 to replace the zipper and salvage the garment. But it's not a difficult alteration to do, and you can learn to replace broken zippers yourself.

Zippers break for a variety of reasons. Determining the exact cause of the problem will help you decide the best way to repair or replace yours.

### Anatomy of a zipper
Pants and skirt zippers have four parts, as shown in the photo on the facing page: the teeth (metal) or coils (plastic), the slide which opens or closes the zipper, the pull or little handle connected to the slide, and the zipper stop, which may be at the top, bottom, or both.

Pulls are generally not replaceable. In 90 percent of instances when the pull comes off the zipper, it's actually the slide underneath that has broken. Also, pulls differ between zipper brands, usually aren't interchangeable, and are nearly impossible to match, particularly if you have owned the garment for a while.

If none of the zipper teeth are missing or bent, the slide can sometimes be replaced. To insert the new slide, however, it is necessary to separate the zipper at the bottom. This repair succeeds only about half the time, usually because it can be difficult to get the slide back on the teeth or coils, or the zipper won't work after the slide is on.

For these reasons, it's almost always best to replace the whole zipper; besides, a new zipper costs only $1 to $1.50, and is available at every fabric and discount store. Currently, manufacturers use plastic zippers for most light- to medium-weight garments because plastic zippers are much stronger than they were in the past. Metal zippers, however, are always used in jeans and heavier garments that require extra strength.

### Steps to follow
The most dreaded replacement is for a zipper in a fly front. Replacement is easy, though, and the step-by-step procedure shown above will guide you through the job. Remember that a women's fly crosses right side over left and a men's fly crosses left over right. The instructions describe the process for a women's garment; reverse the directions for men's pants.

Jeans zippers are more difficult to replace than regular zippers because the fabric is heavier. Use a larger needle size (14 or 16), and sew slowly.

### Preventive maintenance
To avoid future zipper damage, it helps to observe a few simple precautions. Always open the zipper all the way before putting on a garment and close the zipper fully before laundering, which will reduce wear and tear on both the zipper and garment. For sticky zippers, apply a lubricant such as Zipper Ease, which won't stain garments. (To order Zipper Ease, replacement pulls and slides, and zippers of all kinds, contact Oregon Tailor Supply, PO Box 42284, Portland, OR 97242; 503 232-6191.) When you're sewing a new garment, consider using a longer zipper to reduce stress on the teeth or coils during dressing. In place of the usual 7-in. skirt or pants zipper, try a 9-in. one, or cut a 9-in. zipper off at the top to 8 in.    □

*Mary Roehr has written four books on tailoring, including* Altering Women's Ready-to-Wear *and* Altering Men's Ready-to-Wear *(Mansfield, Ohio: Bookmasters Distribution Center, 1988; 800-247-6553). Her article on hemming pants appears on pp. 84-87.*

# The Invisible Zipper

## It's easy to sew and hard to see. Is this the perfect zipper?

*by Carol Neumann*

**d**onna Karan uses it. So does Liz Claiborne and Anne Klein. It even appeared in Betty Ford's 1974 inaugural gown—right up the center front. It's been around for 30 years and is enjoying a welcome comeback.

We're talking about the invisible zipper, and it really is virtually invisible once it's inserted. The only clue that a zipper is hiding under the seam is the streamlined pull tab, as you can see in the photo at right. The zipper is also a breeze to insert, because there's absolutely no topstitching to challenge the sewer or distort the fabric. As a result, it's perfect for fabrics with a lot of surface interest, like sequins, ribbons, or beads. Because it looks just like a seam when closed, this zipper is an excellent choice for fabrics that require careful matching. It can be inserted in any seam, center front, back, or side, and you can use an invisible zipper wherever you'd use an ordinary, non-separating zipper but don't want it to show.

### Meet the zippers

Invisible zippers are sold in the United States by YKK USA (call 404-427-5521 for local distributors; ask for Home Sewing) and Coats & Clark (call 803-234-0331 for local sources; ask for Consumer Services). Both come in lengths from 9 to 22 in. and in many colors, but if you can't find just the right color, you can always paint the pull tab the desired color, since that's all that shows when the zipper's closed. The two brands of zipper are similar enough so that everything said here applies equally to both brands. They can be shortened from the top or the bottom, just like regular zippers (see *Basics, Threads* No. 43, p. 26).

### How they work

Invisible zippers are constructed so that the polyester coils that link together to close the zipper roll to the inside, instead of lying flat as in a regular zipper. You stitch the zipper to the garment fabric right next to the coils, with the coils unrolled. When the coils roll back inside, the fabric pulls together to cover them, as in the top two drawings on the facing page.

To keep the coils unrolled and your stitching accurate during construction, you'll need a special presser foot, like the one in the bottom drawing. Both companies sell a foot for less than $3, complete with instructions and an adapter so it can be used on almost any standard home sewing machine. You can use either brand foot with either zipper. The feet have a slot that fits over the zipper coil and they are fully adjustable left to right, so you can stitch

*We left a little of the seam stitching visible, so you could see where the seam ends and the zipper begins.*

very close to the coil or not, depending on the thickness of the fabric.

To use the zipper foot, attach it to the sewing machine and slide the foot left or right on the adapter until the needle is centered in the needle opening.

## Stitching them in

An invisible zipper is always inserted on the right side of the fabric before any part of the seam is sewn. You stitch it first to one side then to the other in the seam allowances, and then stitch the rest of the seam to meet it.

**Interfacing**—If your fabric is sheer, lightweight, or stretchy, it may need light interfacing to support the weight of the zipper. The completed zipper installation should look just like the pressed-open seam below it: ripple-free and slightly rounded at the seamline. Heavy and tightly woven fabrics typically have enough firmness to stand on their own. Sheers and laces may be interfaced with self-fabric or with cotton or silk organza and lightly glue-basted in position.

Assuming you've got ⅝-in. seam allowances (appropriate for this zipper), interface both zipper seam allowances with a ¾-in.-wide strip of lightweight, fusible interfacing cut on the lengthwise, or most stable, grain. An eighth of an inch of interfacing will extend into the garment.

**Marking**—Begin by marking the zipper position on the right side of the flat garment pieces. Mark where the zipper stops, at the neck or waist stitching line, or the top of an underarm zipper. To make sure you stitch the zipper to the garment exactly on the seam stitching line, I suggest you draw a guideline parallel to it, as in the drawing at right, because you can't see the stitching line when the zipper tape is on top of it. I draw my guideline with a chalk wheel a little less than ⅛ in. from the stitching line into the garment, and line up the coil next to it. Experiment to find the distance that puts your stitching exactly on the stitching line.

**Stitching the zipper**—Open the zipper, unroll the coils, and press the tape (the zipper can take high heat settings) so the coils stand upright away from the tape and will fit into the zipper foot slot. Then position one half of the zipper tape on the corresponding garment piece, right sides together and with the tape on the seam allowance. Pin in place with one pin at the top. The beginning of the coil, or the bar tack if you've shortened it from the top, should be at the top marked line, and the outer edge of the coil should match the

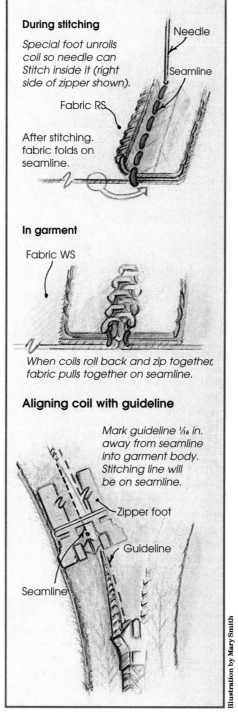

### How invisible zippers work

#### During stitching

*Special foot unrolls coil so needle can Stitch inside it (right side of zipper shown).*

Needle

Seamline

Fabric RS

*After stitching, fabric folds on seamline.*

#### In garment

Fabric WS

*When coils roll back and zip together, fabric pulls together on seamline.*

#### Aligning coil with guideline

*Mark guideline ¹⁄₁₆ in. away from seamline into garment body. Stitching line will be on seamline.*

Zipper foot

Guideline

Seamline

Illustration by Mary Smith

lengthwise guideline. Place the beginning of the coil at the top of a neckline or waistline and you won't need a hook and eye.

Put the top of the coil under the corresponding side of the roller, and start stitching at the top of the tape, unless you have an underarm zipper application; in that case start right at the end of the coil. Heavier fabrics can be stitched in the center needle position. Lighter fabrics may need to be stitched closer to the coil. If necessary, slide the zipper foot on the adapter so the needle is as close as possible to the coil. If in doubt about the correct position,

sew an inch or so, remove the garment from the machine, and try closing the zipper. Even with only one side stitched, it should not bind, nor should the tape be visible between the coil and stitching.

Stitch the length of the coil until the zipper foot touches the pull tab. Be especially careful not to stretch the fabric or the zipper tape while sewing. Allow the zipper foot to act as a third hand; all you need do is guide the coil along the marked guideline. At the tab, lock the stitch by sewing in place several stitches, remove the garment from the machine, and clip the threads.

Close the zipper and mark cross seams, plaids, stripes, etc. on the wrong side of the zipper tape. Open the zipper and pin the free tape to the adjoining garment piece as described above, with the tape in the seam allowance. Position the coil under the other side of the zipper foot and stitch as before, making sure the marks on the tape match the corresponding part of the garment.

**Closing the seam**—Always stitch the rest of the seam with the zipper closed. When close to the zipper, I switch to my regular machine zipper foot, so I can get as close as possible to the zipper stitching at the end of the seam.

Below the zipper, place the garment's right sides together and sew toward the zipper. When you're ½ in. from the zipper coil, shorten the stitch length to 1mm or less, pull the zipper tape toward the right, out from the garment, and sew to the zipper stitches. It's almost impossible to sew exactly over the zipper stitches, so make three to five stitches as close as you can to them, and slightly to the left. If you've got a seam above the zipper, finish it the same way, overlapping as close as possible to the stitches at the start of the coils.

Secure the bottom (and top of an underarm zipper) by stitching the zipper tapes to the seam allowances, so that no stitching shows on the outside. Use the machine zipper foot, and stitch the tape and seam allowance together for about 1 in. on both sides.

Lightly press the closed zipper seam, holding the iron slightly above the right side of the garment, not touching the fabric, and allowing it to steam. Pat the seam gently if necessary, but maintain a slight roll to the seam. If the seam is overpressed, the coil may show through, and your zipper will no longer be invisible. □

*Carol Neumann produces fiber- and fashion-related events. For more information, contact STITCHES, PO Box 832, Lake Elmo, MN 55042.*

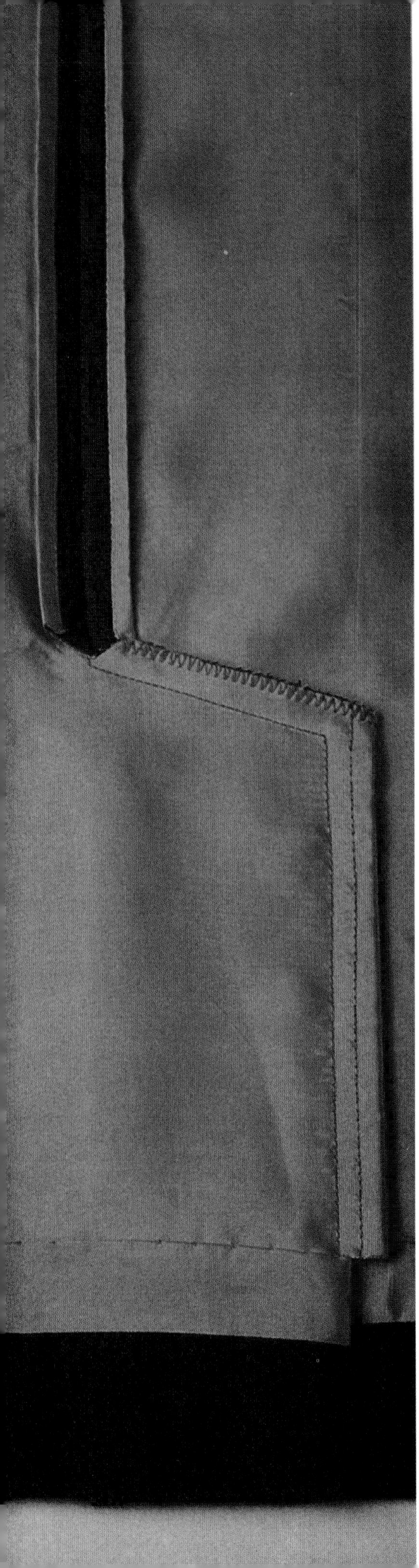

# Flat Lining

## One layer of fabric lines, underlines, and seam finishes skirts and pants

*by Patricia Clements*

*a* few years ago, while recycling a box-pleated A-line skirt into a straight skirt, I read a description of a technique called flat lining. It provides the stability of an underlining, the feel of a lining, and the look of a Hong Kong seam finish, which encloses all raw edges.

My A-line skirt was five years old and had seen regular wear during the winters. The checked wool fabric had stretched out of shape and the grain was distorted. Although I managed to press and pin the fabric back into alignment, I knew the realignment would remain only until the skirt was worn. I also knew that a slip lining, which hangs free inside the skirt, would do little to maintain the garment's shape. Instead, I extended the flat lining technique described in *The Complete Book of Sewing Short Cuts* by Claire B. Shaeffer (Sterling Publishing, New York; 1981).

In this technique, the lining fabric is cut slightly larger at the sides than the garment fabric. The lining fabric is stitched to the garment fabric at the seams, right sides together. When turned right side out, the extra lining fabric wraps around vertical raw edges of the garment fabric. The photo at left shows the inside of a flat-lined garment; the drawings on the facing page show how flat lining works.

Flat lining is suitable any time underlining for stability would be called for—under a loosely woven fabric, for example. In addition to the side, center-front, and center-back seam edges, you can bind the vertical edges of a kick pleat and a straight zipper flap with flat lining. Any thin, smooth lining fabric is appropriate for a flat lining. I always prewash the fabrics, even wool (in warm water and with fabric softener), though I dry-clean the finished wool garments. Make any fitting adjustments to your pattern before cutting the garment and lining fabrics.

### Adding a flat lining

Mark the garment fabric at hipline grainline, center front and back, darts, and notches with tailors' tacks, which will be visible on both right and wrong sides. Cut the garment fabric. Then similarly mark the right side of the lining fabric, using a marker that you have tested to make sure it can be removed later. I often use dressmakers' carbon. Cut the lining fabric, extending by ½ in. each vertical edge—at side seams, center-front and -back seams, and the inner leg seams of pants. This is the extra fabric that will enclose the raw edges of the seam. Do not extend horizontal seams (waist or hem), neckline, crotch, or armscye seams.

Aligning the cut edges and matching notches, stitch the lining fabric of one garment section to the garment fabric along the vertical edges, right sides together, with a ¼-in. seam. Make sure the seams are even and straight.

Turn the garment section right side out. Pin the layers together along the center line or grainline and, with the garment fabric face up, smooth the fabric evenly to the side seams. The lining fabric should curl around the raw edges of the garment section. Check that both layers lie flat, the flat lining turns smoothly over the edges of the garment fabric, and the edges of the garment fabric don't curl. If the lining and fabric don't match, you'll have to restitch them. Lay the pattern on top of the garment section to check that the lined piece is still the same size. If the lining looks good, trim the seam allowances to ⅛ in. for an even smoother fit.

*Purple lining fabric, cut from a skirt's pattern, acts as a slippery underlining and Hong Kong seam-allowance finish for this green wool skirt (inside center-back detail with kick pleat shown at left). A separate strip of lining finishes the hem.*

With the garment section right side out, match and diagonally baste the centers, grainlines, hiplines, and darts. (Diagonal basting, shown at right, keeps the layers from shifting.) Also straight baste the center lines of the darts. Making sure that the now-enclosed edges are smooth and even, press the seam allowances and their "bindings" flat. From the right side, stitch in the ditch to secure the binding. Flat line each garment section in this way. Baste the layers together at the waist, neckline, and hem edges.

## Completing construction

Continue sewing the garment, treating the two layers of fabric as one. Stitch the darts through both garment fabric and flat lining, following the markings on the lining. Sew the vertical seams with an allowance slightly smaller than what the pattern calls for to take into account seam allowances trimmed earlier and to accommodate the added bulk of the flat lining. For example, if the pattern calls for a ⅝-in. allowance, sew one that is ½ in.

For a lapped zipper, cut the zipper seam allowances 1 in. wide. A centered zipper requires no special accommodation.

If the garment has a kick pleat, add the ½-in. extra seam allowance to the flat lining at the center-back seam edges and the vertical edges of the kick pleat, but not to the top edge of the kick pleat. Sew the pleat as usual. Clip the top of this pleat diagonally to the center-back seam. Turn, baste, and press the pleat to one side. Then overcast or zigzag the top edge of the kick pleat. Before hemming, trim seam allowance bulk from within the hem.

## A custom hem binding

For a matching hem tape, I make my own seam binding. I cut 2-in.-wide strips of the garment's lining fabric on the cross grain and make the tape using a 1-in. bias tape maker. I stitch the tape right sides together to the raw edge of the skirt hem, using one fold line of the tape to guide the stitching. I hand stitch the tape to the flat lining only. The resulting hem looks wonderful and is both stable and durable.

In addition to finishing the inside of my recycled wool skirt beautifully, flat lining helped maintain the carefully matched plaid during stitching. Because the lining fabric slides smoothly under the presser foot and the feed dogs don't grab the lining fabric as firmly as they would the wool, the plaid did not distort. And, unlike with slip linings, the back seam has not pulled out. ☐

*Patricia Clements of Nashville, TN, is a former English teacher and longtime sewer.*

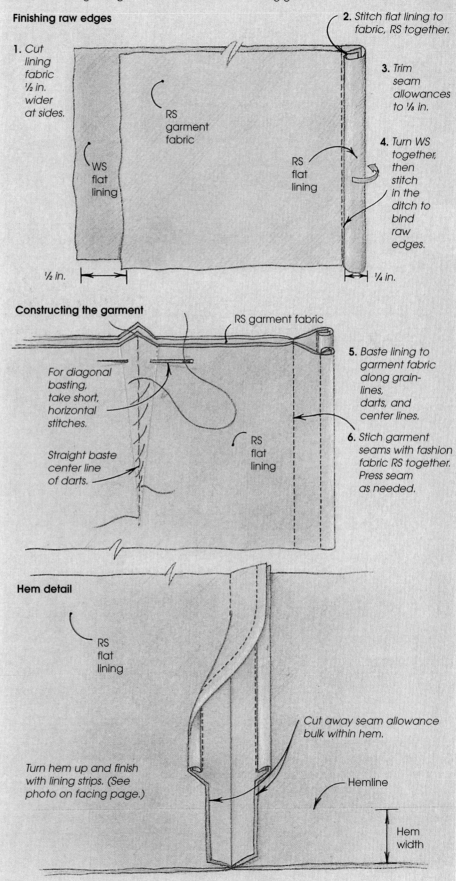

**Flat lining**

*Assemble lining and garment section before seaming garment.*

**Finishing raw edges**

1. Cut lining fabric ½ in. wider at sides.

RS garment fabric

WS flat lining

½ in.

2. Stitch flat lining to fabric, RS together.

3. Trim seam allowances to ⅛ in.

4. Turn WS together, then stitch in the ditch to bind raw edges.

RS flat lining

¼ in.

**Constructing the garment**

RS garment fabric

For diagonal basting, take short, horizontal stitches.

Straight baste center line of darts.

RS flat lining

5. Baste lining to garment fabric along grainlines, darts, and center lines.

6. Stich garment seams with fashion fabric RS together. Press seam as needed.

**Hem detail**

RS flat lining

Turn hem up and finish with lining strips. (See photo on facing page.)

Cut away seam allowance bulk within hem.

Hemline

Hem width

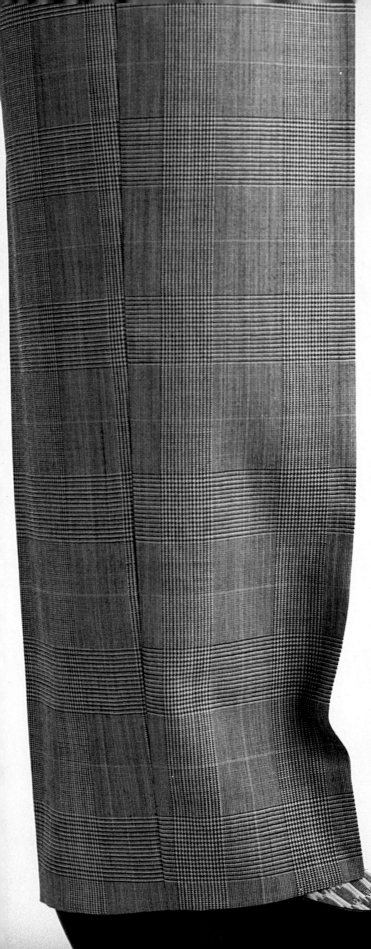

# Getting to the Bottom of Things

Hemming pants is not only a matter of how, but how much

*by Mary A. Roehr*

**O**f all the clothing alterations I do as a tailor, shortening a pants hem is by far the most common, and I'm always amused at my customers' ingenious efforts to do their own hemming before coming for help. Men favor masking tape, duct tape, or staples. Women try less conspicuous options like partially hidden paper clips, safety pins, or awkward, ineffective hand stitching. When time is short, even those of us who sew sometimes look for quick fixes with fusible tape or fabric glue.

I understand the need to save time and I applaud my customers' ingenuity, but it really isn't difficult to successfully shorten a pants hem, even if you don't own a sewing machine. The place to start is deciding how long the pants leg should be.

*The center-front break in the pants hem provides wearing ease and disappears when the knee is bent.*

*A classic 8- to 9-in. pants hem width has a break, or small fold of extra fabric at the instep, and is ¼ to ½ in. lower at center back than center front.*

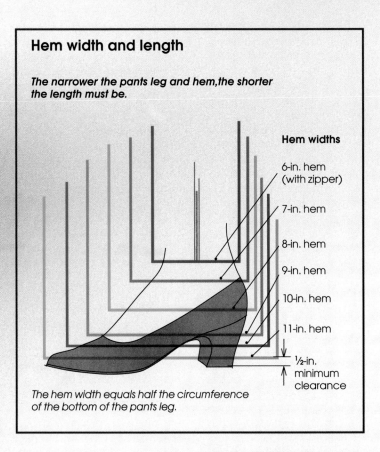

## Hem width and length

*The narrower the pants leg and hem, the shorter the length must be.*

**Hem widths**

6-in. hem
(with zipper)

7-in. hem

8-in. hem

9-in. hem

10-in. hem

11-in. hem

½-in.
minimum
clearance

*The hem width equals half the circumference of the bottom of the pants leg.*

Next you'll need to mark the new hem length and hem allowance, cut off the excess fabric, and finish the raw edge. Then you'll fold, press, and sew the hem, and finish it with a final pressing.

The method described below is the simplest one I know of for shortening the hem on a classic pair of dress pants and should take the average sewer about 30 minutes to an hour to measure and hem both legs. I hope these directions will offer up a tip or two—or at least provide a good review—even for seasoned sewers.

### 1. Determine hem length

The *hem length* is determined by the wearer's preference and the style of the pants (style also establishes the width of the pants hem). In general, the narrower the pants leg and hem, the shorter the length must be since as the hem narrows, it loses the width needed to fall over the top of the foot and shoe (see the drawing above).

*Hem width* is measured with the pants leg laid flat and the measuring tape held straight across the bottom of the leg (see the top drawing on p. 86). This measurement, rather than the full circumference, is traditionally used by tailors and alteration experts in referring to the width of the pants hem. The average hem width for classic business or dress pants for men and women is 8 to 9 in., which allows the pants to cover the ankle and part of the top of the shoe. A hem width of 7 in. or less, usually found on leisurewear, is considered narrow, and a hem narrower than 6 in. usually needs a seamline zipper to allow the foot to pass through. A hem of 10 in. or more is considered full and

*The narrower the hem, the shorter the pants must be. Compare this 5½-in. hem width (slit to allow the foot through) with its classic counterpart on the facing page.*

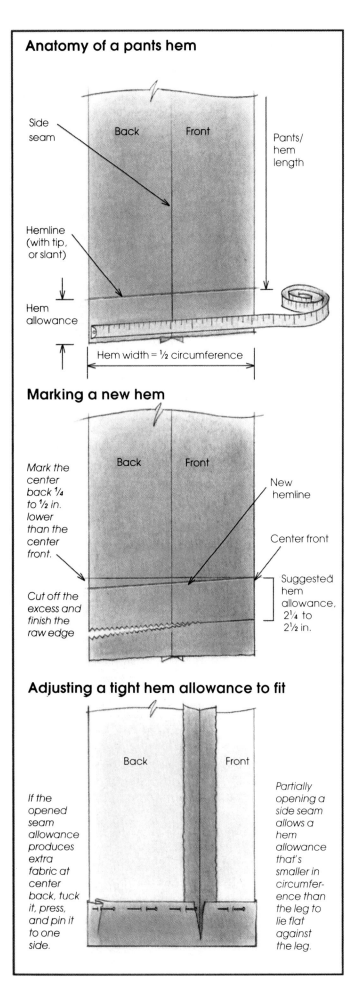

## Anatomy of a pants hem

Side seam

Back · Front

Pants/hem length

Hemline (with tip, or slant)

Hem allowance

Hem width = ½ circumference

## Marking a new hem

Back · Front

Mark the center back ¼ to ½ in. lower than the center front.

New hemline

Center front

Cut off the excess and finish the raw edge

Suggested hem allowance, 2¼ to 2½ in.

## Adjusting a tight hem allowance to fit

Back · Front

If the opened seam allowance produces extra fabric at center back, tuck it, press, and pin it to one side.

Partially opening a side seam allows a hem allowance that's smaller in circumference than the leg to lie flat against the leg.

is termed "bell-bottomed" if the pants leg above is narrow, a style that is recently back in fashion.

When marking the hem length, always mark both legs. Everyone has a slight—and sometimes noticeable—difference in the length of their legs, and marking both pants legs contributes to a custom look and fit (in fact, if you're looking for a good tailor or alterations expert, asking if they mark both legs will tell you a lot about their work). To determine the hem length, decide whether you want the front hem to just touch the top of your shoe or instep or have a *break*, that is, a fold of about ¼ in. of extra fabric over your shoe or instep that vanishes when you walk and bend your knee. The classic 8- to 9-in. pants hem has a small break at center front and is ¼ to ½ in. longer at center back than center front. The slight slope of the hemline, called its *tip*, creates a visually pleasing line and provides wearing ease when the knee is bent (see the inset photo on p. 84).

To decide on the hem length you like, pin up the hem at various lengths using a pin at center front, center back, and each side seam. Be sure to turn the hem under rather than up when you're trying out different lengths. Then when you've decided on the new length, remove all but the pin at center front.

### 2. Mark the hemline

After establishing the new hem length, remove the pants and use tailors' chalk (available at sewing supply stores) to mark the new center-front point of the hem. Then make a second mark at center back ¼ to ½ in. lower than the center-front mark (see the center drawing at left), remove the pin, and rip out the old hem.

Lay the pants on a flat surface with the folds at center front and back, outside leg up. Then, using a ruler as a guide, chalk a line from the center-front mark to the center-back mark. Check again to be sure

that center back is no more than ½ in. lower than center front since a greater tip makes hemming difficult and forms an exaggerated hemline. Then chalk-mark the second side of the new hemline.

Next measure and mark the *hem allowance* all around. To save fabric, clothing manufacturers usually make their hems 1¼ to 1½ in. wide, but the hem will have a little more weight and will drape better if it's 2¼ to 2½ in. wide. This wider hem allowance works for all styles of pants except for leggings, which should have a 1-in.-wide hem, and for jeans, whose ½-in. hem is double turned as well as double stitched.

### 3. Cut off the excess and finish the raw edge

After you've marked the new hemline and hem allowance, cut off the excess and finish the raw edge. Pinking the edge with pinking shears does both jobs at once. Alternatively, you can cut the edge with regular scissors and, if you own a sewing machine, sew hem tape on the edge (or reuse the hem tape if the original hem was taped). To reduce bulk and create a smooth transition, center the width of the tape over the raw edge of the hem allowance and attach the tape with a single row of stitches. Another way to finish the raw edge on the machine is to zigzag the edge. If you have a serger, serging is an excellent way of finishing the edge.

If you don't own a sewing machine or serger, you can nicely finish the edge with Fray Check, a gluelike substance made by Dritz and sold in craft and fabric stores. Apply a thin line to the raw edge of the fabric and allow it to dry thoroughly.

If you're shortening the pants quite a bit, you may find the new hem wider than the original one. If there's more than a 1-in. difference in width between the new and old hems, taper the pants leg so the hem width is the same as the original.

## 4. Fold and press the hem allowance

The next step is to fold under and pin the hem allowance in place, and then press it. Depending on the fabric, the extent of the tip, and the shape of the leg, the turned-up hem may not fit the pants leg exactly. If you're working with a fabric that stretches a little (such as a tweed), the tip is only ¼ in., and the leg doesn't narrow at the hem, then the hem may fit fine. But if your fabric is tightly woven and hasn't much give (like gabardine), the tip is ½ in., and the leg narrows at the hem, you may find the hem smaller in circumference than the leg to which it's to be hemmed.

To give the extra ease needed for the hem to lie flat against the pants leg, rip apart the bottom edge of the side seam and inseam about 1 in. and spread the hem apart slightly at both points (see the bottom drawing on the facing page). After pinning the hem in front, if you find extra fabric at center back, fold a tuck and press and pin it to one side. Then finish pinning the rest of the hem in place.

## 5. Sew the hem

You can sew the hem by machine if your machine has blind-hem or zigzag stitches, or you can hem by hand. My favorite hand-sewing needle for hemming is a size 7 sharp, which pierces the fabric easily and takes small enough bites of fabric as it stitches to keep the stitches invisible on the right side. I recommend this needle for novices, but you can use whatever size you find comfortable.

Work with a length of thread about 24 in. long and knot the end you cut as the thread unwinds from the spool. This helps keep the thread from kinking or knotting because you'll sew with, rather than against, the thread's "grain," or twist. Passing the length of thread once or twice through a cake of beeswax (found at sewing stores) to coat it will also help

prevent it from knotting.

Some people prefer to hem with the running stitch, sometimes called the blind-hemming stitch (see the top drawing at right). I find it easier to hem flat with the catchstitch or whipstitch, both of which, I think, produce more durable hems. All three stitches can be used interchangeably on most fabrics. Whatever stitch you choose, keep your stitches small—just under ¼ in.—and firm but not tight. Pick up only a thread or two on the pants leg as you hem and check to see that the stitches are invisible on the right side of the garment.

## 6. Give the hem a final pressing

A final pressing is a seemingly small detail that can make your hem a great success or a disaster. People tend to slide the iron back and forth across the width of the hem, but working in this direction, across the fabric's grain, can cause the hem to pull diagonally. Always press and lift the iron with the grain of the hem allowance—parallel to the side seam; this will help any extra fabric ease in better and will make your hem lie flat and smooth.

Use steam and a press cloth to prevent scorching the fabric, and always test-press a small section of the hem near the inseam if there's any question about leaving an impression of the hem's finished edge on the right side of the pants. If need be, press just up to, but not over, this edge to avoid an impression. Finally, allow the hem to cool and dry on the ironing board in order to set the press before you hang the pants. □

*Mary Roehr has been a custom tailor for 15 years and has written four books on the subject, including* Altering Women's Ready-to-Wear *and* Altering Men's Ready-to-Wear *(Mansfield, Ohio: Bookmasters Distribution Center, 1988). For ordering information, call (800) 247-6553.*

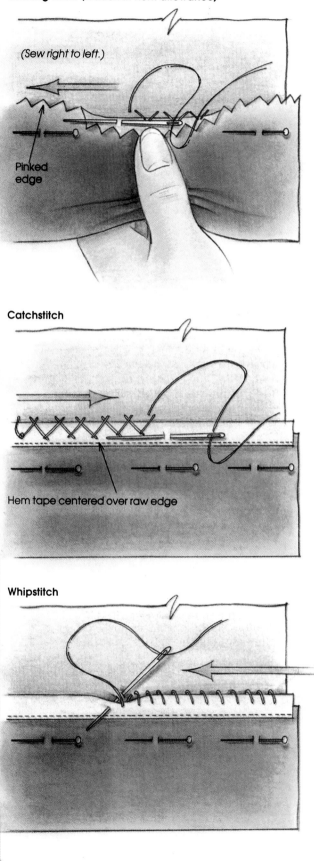

### Hemming by hand
(Hint: *To hide the hemline, catch only one to two fabric threads in each stitch.*)

**Running stitch (hidden in hem allowance)**

(Sew right to left.)

Pinked edge

**Catchstitch**

Hem tape centered over raw edge

**Whipstitch**

# Sewing Room Details

## Threads readers share ideas on cutting tables and storage

by Carol Adney

*Editors' note: In issue No. 36, we asked our readers to tell us about their sewing rooms. We got a blizzard of mail, from folks with dream-come-true rooms, and from those just as happy in make-the-best-of-it cubbyholes. And, of course, every room we were invited to experience, in every letter, was a success; every arrangement was a problem solved.*

*Our problem was to decide which solutions to share with the rest of you. The ideas about work surfaces, storage, and lighting that follow are ideas that others could easily incorporate into their own successful sewing space. We've decided to put the ideas about arranging the space itself in a separate article, to follow soon. Many thanks for the generosity and effort (all those photos, drawings, and floor plans!) of those who sent us ideas. Since most of us at Threads are avid sewers, too, it is a joy to share your pride and enthusiasm.*

When I started reading letters from readers, I expected to see a lot of clever ideas about fabric storage, cutting surfaces, and room arrangement. But your letters weren't only about spaces and hardware—you also shared thoughts and feelings about yourselves, your arts, and how your spaces affected both.

A central theme, voiced over and over again, is *legitimacy*. Many of us connect the validity of what we do with having a designated, recognized place to do it in. Carol Totilo, of Cortlandt Manor, NY, summed it up in her letter: "Serious space tends to give importance to one's work. I could never imagine living where my sewing didn't have as much space as it needed." Marty Burgin, of Dallas, TX, didn't start sewing seriously until she had her room together. For Marianne McCann, of Rochester Hills, MI, the studio is as necessary to her well-being as practicing the fine arts she's trained in.

Peggy Durant, from Clearfield, PA, whose sewing room is shown and described in "An affordable dream room" on p. 92, noted that, while sewing, knitting, spinning, and weaving have always been valid activities to her, her family and friends tend to interrupt her less now that she has a "studio." She says there's less tendency to assume she can put down her work to go do what others want her to be doing.

Along with this sense that a dedicated space makes sewing a serious activity is a second and somewhat paradoxical feeling. Many of us feel isolated and shut out if our work spaces are out of the traffic flow of our families. While the back bedroom may seem to be the perfect place to sew (since we can close the door on the mess), we may still prefer the dining room so that we can fix a snack, mend a

scratch, or just take our inspiration from the life going on around us.

Shirley Johnson Kasprzyk, of Zephyrhills, FL, writes: "I have sewed in the bedroom, in the dining room, and for a while, in an office built in our garage. I thought the office would be perfect, as it had air conditioning, carpeting, phone, and a large drafting table with overhead lighting. But I did not like being so far from the family, so I went back to sewing in the dining room.

"I now have a house with a large family room off the kitchen. The 'breakfast eating area' is now my sewing room. It's perfect, as I can see television, be with the family, and am near the kitchen and utility room."

An architect who listened has Carol Sperling's eternal gratitude for designing a sewing room adjacent to her kitchen in Eveleth, MN. While her children were growing up she could sew, keep watch on dinner, and make sure no one drowned in the lake. "Mother is the center of the home," she told me, and she loved staying in the center.

The back bedroom of Leora Emerson's mobile home in Avila Beach, CA, had been her sewing room for years, but she describes it as cold and dark, and the carpet as a magnet for pins which then found her husband's feet. Her new sewing room, built off the kitchen, is "the dream of my life." Her fold-away table is shown in the drawing on the facing page. When I asked her what role the sewing room played in her life, she called it "the heart of the house."

## Cutting tables

The most important part of the sewing room is the sewing machine, right? Not according to the responses we received. Nearly half of the letters concerned cutting surfaces, some to the exclusion of

From *Threads* magazine (December 1992) 44:54-59

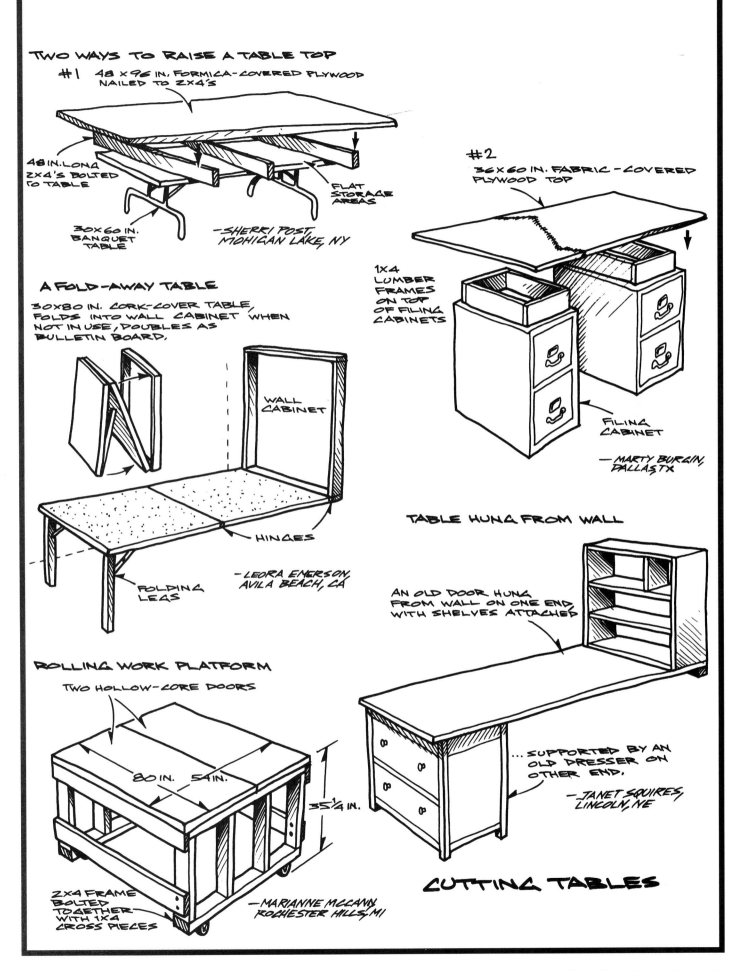

# TWO WAYS TO RAISE A TABLE TOP

#1 48 x 96 IN. FORMICA-COVERED PLYWOOD NAILED TO 2x4's

48 IN. LONG 2x4's BOLTED TO TABLE

FLAT STORAGE AREAS

30x60 IN. BANQUET TABLE

—SHERRI POST, MICHIGAN LAKE, NY

#2

36x60 IN. FABRIC-COVERED PLYWOOD TOP

1x4 LUMBER FRAMES ON TOP OF FILING CABINETS

FILING CABINET

—MARTY BURGIN, DALLAS, TX

## A FOLD-AWAY TABLE

30x80 IN. CORK-COVER TABLE, FOLDS INTO WALL CABINET WHEN NOT IN USE, DOUBLES AS BULLETIN BOARD.

WALL CABINET

HINGES

FOLDING LEGS

— LEORA EMERSON, AVILA BEACH, CA

## TABLE HUNG FROM WALL

AN OLD DOOR HUNG FROM WALL ON ONE END WITH SHELVES ATTACHED

...SUPPORTED BY AN OLD DRESSER ON OTHER END.

—JANET SQUIRES, LINCOLN, NE

## ROLLING WORK PLATFORM

TWO HOLLOW-CORE DOORS

80 IN.   54 IN.

35¼ IN.

2x4 FRAME BOLTED TOGETHER WITH 1x4 CROSS PIECES

—MARIANNE McCANN, ROCHESTER HILLS, MI

# CUTTING TABLES

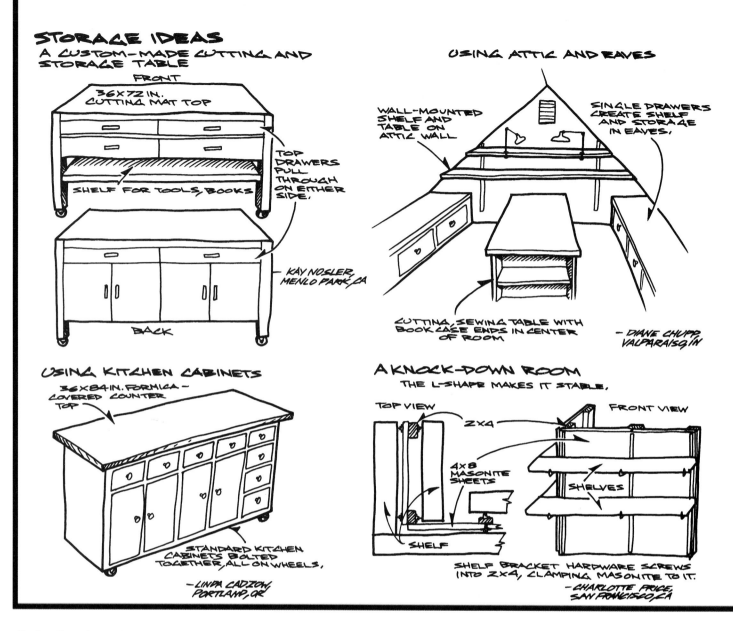

## STORAGE IDEAS

### A CUSTOM-MADE CUTTING AND STORAGE TABLE

FRONT

36 X 72 IN. CUTTING MAT TOP

TOP DRAWERS PULL THROUGH ON EITHER SIDE.

SHELF FOR TOOLS, BOOKS

BACK

— KAY NOSLER, MENLO PARK, CA

### USING ATTIC AND EAVES

WALL-MOUNTED SHELF AND TABLE ON ATTIC WALL

SINGLE DRAWERS CREATE SHELF AND STORAGE IN EAVES.

CUTTING, SEWING TABLE WITH BOOK CASE ENDS IN CENTER OF ROOM

— DIANE CHUPP, VALPARAISO, IN

### USING KITCHEN CABINETS

36 X 84 IN. FORMICA-COVERED COUNTER TOP

STANDARD KITCHEN CABINETS BOLTED TOGETHER, ALL ON WHEELS.

— LINDA CADZOW, PORTLAND, OR

### A KNOCK-DOWN ROOM

THE L-SHAPE MAKES IT STABLE.

TOP VIEW

FRONT VIEW

2 X 4

4 X 8 MASONITE SHEETS

SHELVES

SHELF

SHELF BRACKET HARDWARE SCREWS INTO 2X4, CLAMPING MASONITE TO IT.

— CHARLOTTE PRICE, SAN FRANCISCO, CA

---

all else. Drawings of some useful tables, from the do-it-yourself to the custom-made, are shown on p. 89 and above.

Why do we love our tables above all else? When I called readers to ask them more, I got a series of increasingly enlightening responses. Terry Cronan Hollowell, from Woodland, CA, loves her table because it's the only thing she has that's devoted only to sewing. It's shown on the facing page. Anne Bartley, of Nepean, ON, Canada said that it's because we spend relatively little time at the machine compared to the time spent laying out and cutting.

Marianne McCann's got one of the biggest tables we heard about; it's shown on p. 89. She told me that her work table was the most important part of her studio because the creative process begins at the table. For her, the exciting part of sewing is exploring the possibilities inherent in the project, the interaction be-

tween her hands and eyes and the fabric. Assembling, to her, is the work that gets done after most of the creating has already happened.

**Dimensions**—Our tables' lengths and widths vary according to space available, but most of us want a table at counter height or higher, between 35 and 36 in. For most of us, this reduces back strain while still allowing for a reach across the table. At 5 ft. 6 in. tall, I've found heights up to 40 in. comfortable, if I could walk around two long sides of the table.

Raising a too-low table is no problem. Dorothy Fusselman, of Chagrin Falls, OH, extended her banquet table's legs with precut lengths of metal pipe from the hardware store. The wide range of pipe diameters available made it easy to find just the right width to slip over the legs.

Robin Brisco, from Tustin, CA, wanted to use a pair of teak end tables in her

sewing room, but they were too short to support a top until she hit on the idea of stacking several tops on them. She had three plywood layers made; two are Formica-covered, and the top one's padded, and all have carefully rounded corners. Then she gathered 4-in.-thick blocks of wood from her husband's wood shop, covered each with felt, and slipped them between the layers to separate them and support the centers and corners. The spaces in between form ample storage areas for large flat things, shallow boxes, and the single wide, wooden drawer her husband added that's just the right height for pull-out convenience.

**Coverings**—The only real difference of opinion regarding the cutting table centers on the nature of the surface. We're almost evenly split between fans of the smooth, hard surface and devotees of the softer, upholstered surface.

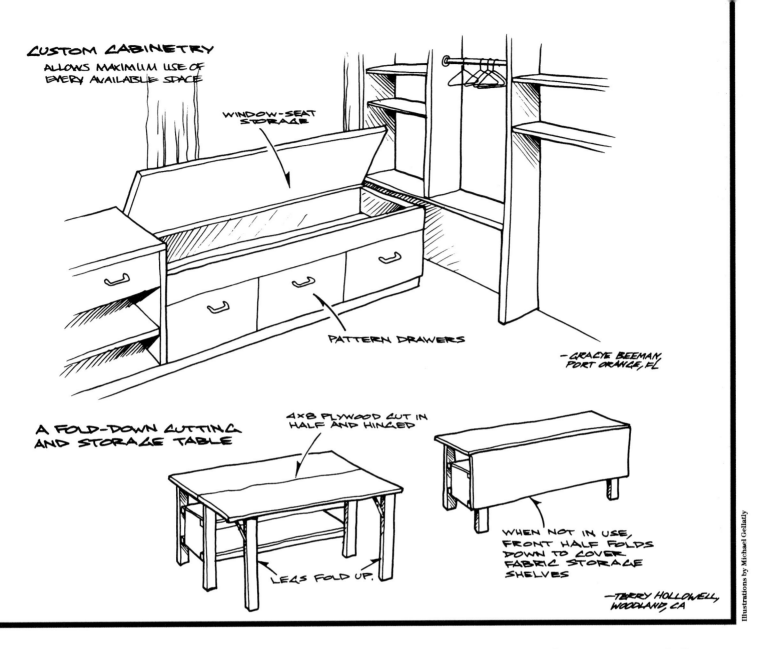

CUSTOM CABINETRY ALLOWS MAXIMUM USE OF EVERY AVAILABLE SPACE

WINDOW-SEAT STORAGE

PATTERN DRAWERS

—GRACIE BEEMAN, PORT ORANGE, FL

A FOLD-DOWN CUTTING AND STORAGE TABLE

4×8 PLYWOOD CUT IN HALF AND HINGED

LEGS FOLD UP.

WHEN NOT IN USE, FRONT HALF FOLDS DOWN TO COVER FABRIC STORAGE SHELVES

—TERRY HOLLOWELL, WOODLAND, CA

Illustrations by Michael Gellatly

A hard surface has the advantage of allowing your scissors to glide smoothly on the table under the fabric as you cut. Finishes that were suggested for this were several coats of high-gloss enamel paint, Formica, and bathroom-type wallboard with a glossy finish. I prefer to use tempered hardboard, like Masonite, because of its warmer feel. If its hard surface gets scratched with use, as will happen in time, it is also inexpensive and easy to replace.

Many seamsters prefer a fabric-covered table. After cushioning the table with batting, wool blankets, or carpet padding, they cover it with canvas or duck, stretched on top and stapled into the back. This allows them to pin into the surface, keeps fabric from sliding around on the table, and gives them an ultra-large pressing surface if they need it.

Of course, if you do most of your cutting with a rotary cutter and a storable cutting mat, as many seamsters do nowadays, a smooth table top may not be that important. Threads editor David Coffin takes the opposite approach. He says that he'd never sew without his table-sized rotary-cutting mat permanently installed. Whenever he's pressing new yardage, he whips out a 34- by 56-in. padded board from behind the door, supporting the board's front edge at a comfortable standing height with his ironing board, while the back edge rests on stacked books on his table behind.

## Storage

The second largest category of responses from readers concerned storage. Some seamsters out there actually say that they buy only what they intend to make up next, and that they store nothing. Most of us, however, have gained the courage to face our dependency squarely and admit that we hoard fabric, patterns, trims, buttons, zippers, and all manner of other important items. The only problem with having everything is: Where to put it all?

**Shelves**—I read somewhere recently that the best way to store fabric is in cardboard boxes. Just sort your fabric, the author said, label the boxes, and put them away. Well, I did that for years. It would be stretching the point to say that the day I got my fabric collection out of boxes was the happiest day of my life, but not by much.

For about the same amount of money as I would have paid for those industrial, gray, sharp-edged, ten-thousand-bolted, wobbly garage shelves (about $27), I found what I think is a seamster's dream come true. I got a shelf unit three feet wide, six feet high, and a foot deep and sturdy enough to load completely with folded fabric. Each shelf has a 5⁄8-in. lip

# An affordable dream room

*by Peggy Durant*

*When she had little room for sewing, Peggy Durant made little time to use it and felt she was stealing space from her family. But an attic remodel opened up plenty of space for other family members, so she finally had a room to call her own. Following is the story of her new, guilt-free room, shown in the photo on the facing page.—C.A.*

**W**ith my family adequately situated, I no longer felt guilty about the amount of space that my equipment was taking up. (By now I had accumulated a new sewing machine, a serger, two knitting machines, a linker, two spinning wheels, a floor loom, an industrial iron, a drum carder, and an unwieldy supply of fabrics, fibers, yarns, books, and magazines.) The unofficial sewing/laundry/guest room became officially mine in which to design a sewing/knitting studio. With the loom, spinning wheels, and other spinning/weaving paraphernalia occupying one wing of the new family room in the attic, my task was to design efficient working space for my sewing, knitting, laundry, and supplies.

Since I have two knitting machines, the first and easiest decision was the purchase of a Keyto dual-tilt knitting-machine table designed to hold two machines back-to-back with a storage bin between the machines. It was soft gray in color, so I chose a neutral light and medium gray as colors for my flooring, walls, and woodwork. I had 10- and 12-in.-wide gray wood shelving installed on every possible space on the four walls of the room.

Shopping for sewing furniture was frustrating. What I could find was expensive, generally poor quality, and designed for sewers who want to put everything out of sight after each sewing session. Since I was devoting an entire room to fiber work, I wanted good-looking, functional furniture that would allow me free access to my machines at all times. My solution was to use computer and office furniture in unique ways.

My sewing table is a 24- by 48-in. computer desk with a pull-out keyboard shelf under the right end of the table. I had a hole cut in the top of the desk, over the keyboard tray, and placed my Bernina machine in the hole. It rests on the keyboard tray and the detachable flatbed covers the hole, resting on the table surface. The flatbed cover removes easily for using the free arm or changing bobbins. The Bernina knee control sticks out between the tray and the table top.

My cutting table consists of a 30- by 60-in. desk top ordered from our local office supply store. I bought metal workbench legs at the hardware store that were long enough to put the table top 35 in. above the floor, and had a handyman attach them to the top. He also added braces in back to add stability.

The cost of the furniture was moderate: three pieces of computer furniture for about $229, Keyto table for $250 (on sale), and desk top for $80. Shelving supplies and labor to install were about $600, but that includes having all the shelf boards cut to length at the lumber yard. The total cost of the room fixtures was less than $1500, installed.

One of dozens of sewing rooms Threads readers wrote to tell us about, Peggy Durant's dream sewing and machine-knitting room was outfitted almost exclusively with standard hardware and office furniture, not costly, specialized sewing equipment.

---

all the way around, so my fabric doesn't slide off. There are no rough edges to snag fabric, it snaps together without tools, and since it's a non-brittle plastic, I don't worry about it rusting.

My shelves are made in the U.S.A. by Contico, and come in white, beige, and blue. Contico also makes organizers, crates, and tool boxes from high-tech plastics. They're available at Wal-Mart and other stores.

Another great-looking shelving unit was suggested to us by Dorothy Fusselman. It's called Tic Tac shelving, and it's available from Conran's Habitat (call 800-3-CONRANS for the store nearest you—they're located mostly on the East and West coasts). Eighteen square compartments look like they'd hold fabric and other items (yarn?) nicely. The unit is 79 in. high, 38 in. wide, and 13 in. deep. It cost Dorothy $185 and weighs in at 152 lbs.

**Under the table**—One area of "wasted" space that most of us convert to storage is under our cutting tables. Several readers sent ideas for combination cutting table/storage units, shown on pgs. 90 and 91. Others suggested putting bookshelves or file cabinets under the table.

Taking my cue from these readers, I made a major change in my sewing room. Instead of adding height to my banquet table with bricks or pipes, I folded its legs and put it on top of the dresser I use to store patterns, interfacings, cutting tools, and miscellaneous craft items. It just fit on top, and a decorative trim strip on the dresser fortuitously keeps the table from sliding. It's just shy of 35 in. high—about 2 in. lower than my optimum—but for a no-work, no-cash idea, it's great.

**Bins**—Brother Antonine Correa of the Old Mission in Santa Barbara, CA, who embellishes liturgical garments and makes wall hangings, built a storage wall for his appliqué fabrics from three-gallon ice cream cartons stacked together on their sides. After taping them together, he filled the fronts of the spaces in between the round cartons with papier-mâché. A coat of white paint finished his organizer wall, which he keeps stocked with fabric sorted by color family. You can sometimes get the empty cartons from your local ice cream store.

Janet Squires, from Lincoln, NE, stores what she calls odds and ends (elastic, zippers, shoulder pads, ribbon, lace, boning) in oatmeal containers stacked on their sides in a small-sized variation of Bro. Antonine's wall. Hers are stacked loose in a bookcase, and have labels on their covers. Barbara Hovagian's dream remodel in Tucson, AZ, includes tilt-out storage bins alongside the kneeholes at each sewing machine for dumping scraps of fabric and interfacing.

**Opposite extremes**—There's storage, and then there's storage. For Gloria Robinson, in Chicago, IL, it's essential to put everything away at the end of each sewing session, not just at the end of a project. She bought a put-it-together-yourself (knock-down) wardrobe, which she uses to store her entire sewing room. Her folding sewing-machine table, as well as her machine, ironing board, and all other materials, fits inside. When she gets home from work, her apartment is neat as a pin, which she says inspires her to begin sewing again.

In order *not* to have to clean up in the middle of a project, Charlotte Price, of San Francisco, CA, created a make-it-yourself room, which has traveled with her through 20 years of apartments. Assembled out of of 8-ft. 2x4's and three wallpaper-covered 4- by 8-in. sheets of Masonite, her two portable "walls" form an "L" to support each other, and conceal

a 4- by 10-ft. sewing space, which is just large enough for a machine table and storage shelves. On the outside, more shelves hold books. The drawing on p. 90 shows how it fits together.

## Lighting and power

Track lighting was the favorite of our readers. Aiming overhead light directly on their work made their lives much more pleasant. Those of us without track lighting generally make do with swing arm lamps or overhead incandescents. A few were happy with fluorescent lighting, but some questioned the color distortion they create. Quilter Elaine Spencer, from Fort Collins, CO, installed both incandescent and color-corrected fluorescent, so she can compare the color effects in various combinations of lighting.

When Dee Hiller, of San Diego, CA, added almost 500 square feet to her house in the form of a sewing room over

the garage, the electrical supply was a major concern. Track lights over her cutting table and recessed lights at each end of the room provide ample candle power. She installed Wiremold (available from building supply houses), which allows electric supply wiring to be attached to the surface of a wall, rather than pulled through a wall. Dee put lines around all the walls close to the floor, with receptacles every 12 inches. She also had three duplex receptacles installed in the floor. Proceeding despite the neighbors' disparaging remarks, Dee was vindicated when her needlework group plugged in machines and irons and didn't blow a single fuse. As is the case with all the readers who wrote to us, Dee's sewing room room reflects her own unique priorities. □

---

*Carol Adney's article on sewing without pins appears on pp. 39-41.*

# Index

**A**

Adney, Carol:
    on sewing rooms, 88-93
    on sewing without pins, 39-41
Awl, using, 19-21

**B**

Bias:
    binding with, 60-63
    establishing true, 61
    working with, 52-55
Bindings, bias, 60-63
Buttonholes:
    cording, 69
    in silk, 66-69

**C**

Clements, Patricia, on flat lining for
    skirts and pants, 82-83
Closures:
    button loop, 62
    *See also* Zippers.
Coffin, David Page:
    on rotary cutters for
        garmentmaking, 26-29
    on thread facts and sources, 33
    on turning points, 56-59
Collar, points, 56-59
Cutting tools, rotary cutters, 26-29

**D**

Davies, Diana, on serging knits,
    22-25
Durant, Peggy, on sewing room, 92

**E**

Ease, in patterns, 46-49

**F**

Fabric:
    amount required for turning
        edges, 50-51
    cutting tools for, 26-29
    drape of, and ease, 46-49
    knit, serging, 22-25
    preparing for sewing, 36-38
Faiola, Linda, on changing seam
    allowances, 42-45
Fouché, Shermane, on shaping
    sleeve cap, 64-65

**G**

Gale, Joyce, on working with bias,
    52-55
Gathers, by machine, 17
Grainlines, how to find and
    straighten, 36-38

**H**

Hazen, Gale Grigg:
    on determining ease needed,
        46-49
    on marking seam allowances, 45
    on perfecting the straight stitch,
        12-15
    on sewing-machine technique,
        16-18
    on testing a sewing machine, 10
    on thread, 30-32
Hems, on pants, shortening, 84-87

**I**

Interfacings:
    low-temp., 34-35, 67
    sources for, 69

**J**

Jacket, shaping sleeve cap for, 64-65

**K**

Komives, Margaret, on low-temp.
    fusibles, 34-35

**M**

Meyrich, Elissa:
    on using an awl when machine
        sewing, 19-21
    on zipper insertion, 75-77
Morris, Karen, on choosing a sewing
    machine, 8-11

**N**

Necklines, bias bindings for, 60-61
Neumann, Carol, on invisible
    zippers, 80-81

**P**

Pants, hemming, 84-87
Pockets, welt, 70-74
Points, turning, 56-59

**R**

Roehr, Mary A.:
    on hemming pants, 84-87
    on replacing a zipper, 78-79
Rotary cutters. *See* Cutting tools.

**S**

Seam allowances:
    changing, 42-45
    marking, 45
Serging:
    knits, 22-25
    stitches with, 22-23
Sewing, machine:
    buttonholes, 66-69
    flat lining for skirts and pants,
        82-83
    without pins, 39-41
    points, turning, 56-59
    preparing fabric for, 36-38
    staystitching template for, 62
    straight stitching, perfecting,
        12-15
Sewing machines:
    choosing, 8-11
    improving technique on, 16-18
    testing, 10
Sewing notions:
    awl, 19-21
    cutting mats, 27, 28-29
    interfacings, low-temp., 34-35
    tools for point turning, 58
    trolley needle, 21
    *See also* Cutting tools.
Sewing rooms, tips from readers,
    88-93
Shaeffer, Claire B.:
    on bias binding, 60-63
    on buttonholes in silk, 66-69
Silk:
    interfacings for, 67
    making buttonholes in, 66-69
Sleeve:
    caps, shaping, 64-65
    setting without pins, 40, 41
Smith, Shirley:
    on fabric required for turn of the
        cloth, 50-51
    on preparing fabric for sewing,
        36-38

**T**

Thread:
    facts about, 30-33
    sources for, 33, 69
Turn of the cloth, fabric required for,
    50-51

**W**

Wakefield, Linda, on welt pockets,
    70-74
Wolf, Colette, on trolley needle, 21

**Z**

Zippers:
    inserting, 75-77
    invisible, 80-81
    replacing, 78-79

Look for these and other *Threads* books at your local bookstore
or sewing retailer.

For a catalog of the complete line of *Threads* books and videos, write to
The Taunton Press, P.O. Box 5506, Newtown, CT 06470-5506.